HAMMOND

Atlas of United States History

Mapmakers for the 21st Century

Contents

REVISED 2001 EDITION

ENTIRE CONTENTS © COPYRIGHT MCMXCVII BY HAMMOND WORLD ATLAS CORPORATION

All rights reserved. No part of this book may be reproduced or utilized in any form or by any means, electronic or mechanical, including photocopying, recording or by any information storage and retrieval system, without permission in writing from the Publisher.

LIBRARY OF CONGRESS CATALOG CARD NUMBER 96-49621

ISBN 0-8437-1761-0 (sc)

ISBN 0-8437-1449-2 (hc)

PRINTED IN THE UNITED STATES OF AMERICA

Gazetteer of States, Territories and Possessions

State or Territory	Area (sq. mi.)†	Area (sq. km.)†	Population (2000)	Inhabitants per sq. mi. ††	Admitted to the Union	Settled at	Date
Alabama	52,237	135,293	4,447,100 *23*	87.6	Dec. 14, 1819	Mobile	1702
Alaska	615,230	1,593,444	626,932 *48*	1.1	Jan. 3, 1959	Sitka	1801
American Samoa	90	233	(65,446§)	849.9	*Feb. 16, 1900	....	....
Arizona	114,006	295,276	5,130,632 *20*	45.1	Feb. 14, 1912	Tucson	1752
Arkansas	53,182	137,742	2,673,400 *33*	51.3	Jun. 15, 1836	Arkansas Post	1685
California	158,869	411,470	33,871,648 *1*	217.2	Sept. 9, 1850	San Diego	1769
Colorado	104,100	269,618	4,301,261 *24*	41.5	Aug. 1, 1876	Near Denver	1858
Connecticut	5,544	14,358	3,405,565 *29*	702.9	Jan. 9, 1788	Windsor	1635
Delaware	2,396	6,206	783,600 *45*	400.8	Dec. 7, 1787	Cape Henlopen	1627
District of Columbia	68	177	572,059 *50*	9,378.0	** 1790-1791	....	1790
Florida	59,928	155,214	15,982,378 *4*	296.3	Mar. 3, 1845	St. Augustine	1565
Georgia	58,977	152,750	8,186,453 *10*	141.3	Jan. 2, 1788	Savannah	1733
Guam	217	561	(154,623§)	736.3	*Dec. 10, 1898	Agana	1668
Hawaii	6,459	16,729	1,211,537 *42*	188.6	Aug. 21, 1959	....	....
Idaho	83,574	216,456	1,293,953 *39*	15.6	July 3, 1890	Coeur d'Alene	1842
Illinois	57,918	150,007	12,419,293 *5*	223.4	Dec. 3, 1818	Kaskaskia	1720
Indiana	36,420	94,328	6,080,485 *14*	169.5	Dec. 11, 1816	Vincennes	1730
Iowa	56,276	145,754	2,926,324 *30*	52.4	Dec. 28, 1846	Burlington	1788
Kansas	82,282	213,110	2,688,418 *32*	32.9	Jan. 29, 1861	....	1831
Kentucky	40,411	104,665	4,041,769 *25*	101.7	June 1, 1792	Harrodsburg	1774
Louisiana	49,651	128,595	4,468,976 *22*	102.6	Apr. 30, 1812	Iberville	1699
Maine	33,741	87,388	1,274,923 *40*	41.3	Mar. 15, 1820	Bristol	1624
Maryland	12,297	31,849	5,296,486 *19*	541.8	Apr. 28, 1788	St. Mary's	1634
Massachusetts	9,241	23,934	6,349,097 *13*	810.0	Feb. 6, 1788	Plymouth	1620
Michigan	96,705	250,465	9,938,444 *8*	174.9	Jan. 26, 1837	Near Detroit	1650
Minnesota	86,943	225,182	4,919,479 *21*	61.8	May 11, 1858	St. Peter's River	1805
Mississippi	48,268	125,060	2,844,658 *31*	60.6	Dec. 10, 1817	Natchez	1716
Missouri	69,709	180,546	5,595,211 *17*	81.2	Aug. 10, 1821	St. Louis	1764
Montana	147,046	380,849	902,195 *44*	6.2	Nov. 8, 1889	....	1809
Nebraska	77,358	200,358	1,711,263 *38*	22.3	Mar. 1, 1867	Bellevue	1847
Nevada	110,567	286,367	1,998,257 *35*	18.2	Oct. 31, 1864	Genoa	1850
New Hampshire	9,283	24,044	1,235,786 *41*	137.8	June 21, 1788	Dover and Portsmouth	1623
New Jersey	8,215	21,277	8,414,350 *9*	1,134.2	Dec. 18, 1787	Bergen	1617
New Mexico	121,598	314,939	1,819,046 *36*	15.0	Jan. 6, 1912	Santa Fe	1605
New York	53,989	139,833	18,976,457 *3*	401.8	July 26, 1788	Manhattan Island	1614
North Carolina	52,672	136,421	8,049,313 *11*	165.2	Nov. 21, 1789	Albemarle	1650
North Dakota	70,704	183,123	642,200 *47*	9.3	Nov. 2, 1889	Pembina	1780
Northern Marianas	189	490	(71,912§)	401.7	Apr. 2, 1947	....	....
Ohio	44,828	116,103	11,353,140 *7*	277.2	Mar. 1, 1803	Marietta	1788
Oklahoma	69,903	181,048	3,450,654 *27*	50.2	Nov. 16, 1907	....	1889
Oregon	97,132	251,571	3,421,399 *28*	35.6	Feb. 14, 1859	Astoria	1810
Pennsylvania	46,058	119,291	12,281,054 *6*	274.0	Dec. 12, 1787	Delaware River	1682
Puerto Rico	3,508	9,085	(3,808,610)	1,111.4	*Dec. 10, 1898	Caparra	1510
Rhode Island	1,231	3,189	1,048,319 *43*	1,003.2	May 29, 1790	Providence	1636
South Carolina	31,189	80,779	4,012,012 *26*	133.2	May 23, 1788	Port Royal	1670
South Dakota	77,121	199,744	754,844 *46*	9.9	Nov. 2, 1889	Sioux Falls	1856
Tennessee	42,146	109,158	5,689,283 *16*	138.0	June 1, 1796	Ft. Loudon	1757
Texas	267,277	692,248	20,851,820 *2*	79.6	Dec. 29, 1845	Matagorda Bay	1686
Utah	84,904	219,902	2,233,169 *34*	27.2	Jan. 4, 1896	Salt Lake City	1847
Vermont	9,615	24,903	608,827 *49*	65.8	Mar. 4, 1791	Ft. Dummer	1764
Virginia	42,326	109,625	7,078,515 *12*	178.8	June 26, 1788	Jamestown	1607
Virgin Islands	171	443	(120,917§)	7,902.3	*Mar 31, 1917	St. Thomas I.	1657
Washington	70,637	182,949	5,894,121 *15*	88.5	Nov. 11, 1889	Astoria	1811
West Virginia	24,231	62,759	1,808,344 *37*	75.1	June 20, 1863	Wheeling	1774
Wisconsin	65,499	169,643	5,363,675 *18*	98.8	May 29, 1848	Green Bay	1670
Wyoming	97,818	253,349	493,782 *51*	5.1	July 10, 1890	Ft. Laramie	1834
United States	3,717,796	9,629,091	281,421,906	79.6	....	....	....
United States, Territories & Possessions	3,721,971	9,639,903	285,643,414	80.7	....	....	....

* Date of organization as Territory or acquisition by U.S. ** Established under Acts of Congress † Land and water. †† Calculations based on land area.
§ Estimated population

Source: US Census Bureau

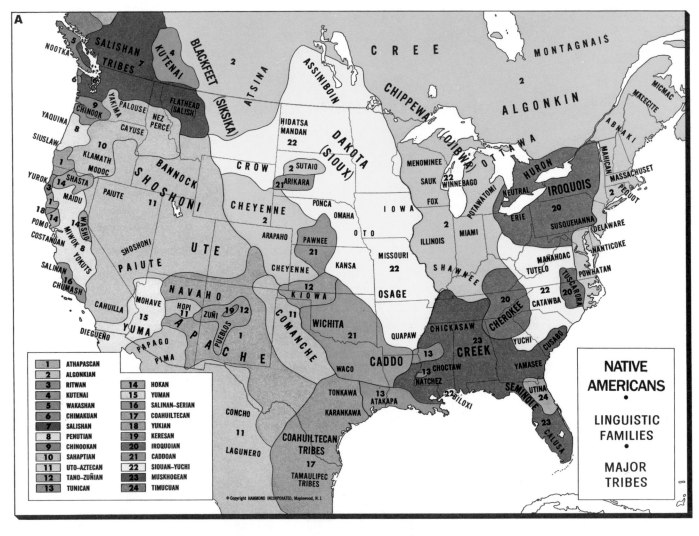

A

NATIVE AMERICANS
•
LINGUISTIC FAMILIES
•
MAJOR TRIBES

1 ATHAPASCAN	
2 ALGONKIAN	
3 RITWAN	14 HOKAN
4 KUTENAI	15 YUMAN
5 WAKASHAN	16 SALINAN–SERIAN
6 CHIMAKUAN	17 COAHUILTECAN
7 SALISHAN	18 YUKIAN
8 PENUTIAN	19 KERESAN
9 CHINOOKAN	20 IROQUOIAN
10 SAHAPTIAN	21 CADDOAN
11 UTO–AZTECAN	22 SIOUAN–YUCHI
12 TANO–ZUÑIAN	23 MUSKHOGEAN
13 TUNICAN	24 TIMUCUAN

© Copyright HAMMOND INCORPORATED, Maplewood, N. J.

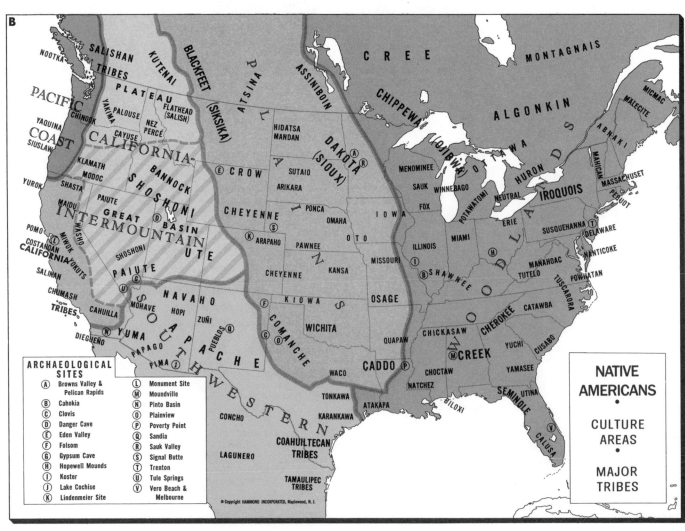

B

NATIVE AMERICANS
•
CULTURE AREAS
•
MAJOR TRIBES

ARCHAEOLOGICAL SITES

Ⓐ	Browns Valley & Pelican Rapids	Ⓛ	Monument Site
Ⓑ	Cahokia	Ⓜ	Moundville
Ⓒ	Clovis	Ⓝ	Pinto Basin
Ⓓ	Danger Cave	Ⓞ	Plainview
Ⓔ	Eden Valley	Ⓟ	Poverty Point
Ⓕ	Folsom	Ⓠ	Sandia
Ⓖ	Gypsum Cave	Ⓡ	Sauk Valley
Ⓗ	Hopewell Mounds	Ⓢ	Signal Butte
Ⓘ	Koster	Ⓣ	Trenton
Ⓙ	Lake Cochise	Ⓤ	Tule Springs
Ⓚ	Lindenmeier Site	Ⓥ	Vero Beach & Melbourne

© Copyright HAMMOND INCORPORATED, Maplewood, N. J.

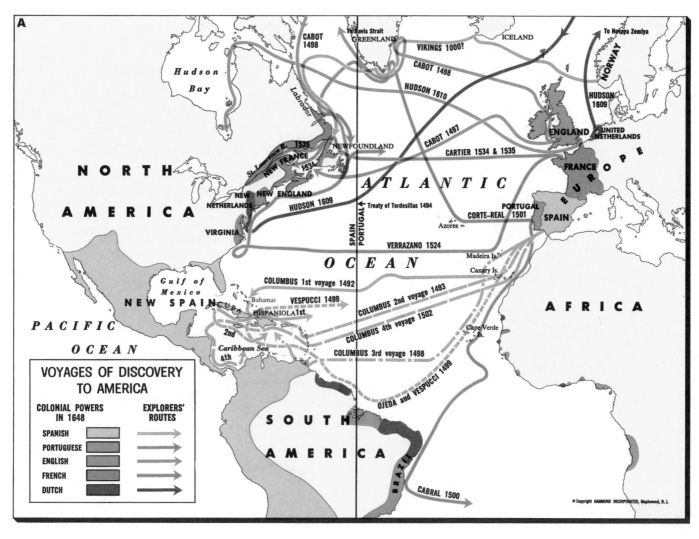

A

VOYAGES OF DISCOVERY TO AMERICA

COLONIAL POWERS IN 1648 — EXPLORERS' ROUTES

SPANISH
PORTUGUESE
ENGLISH
FRENCH
DUTCH

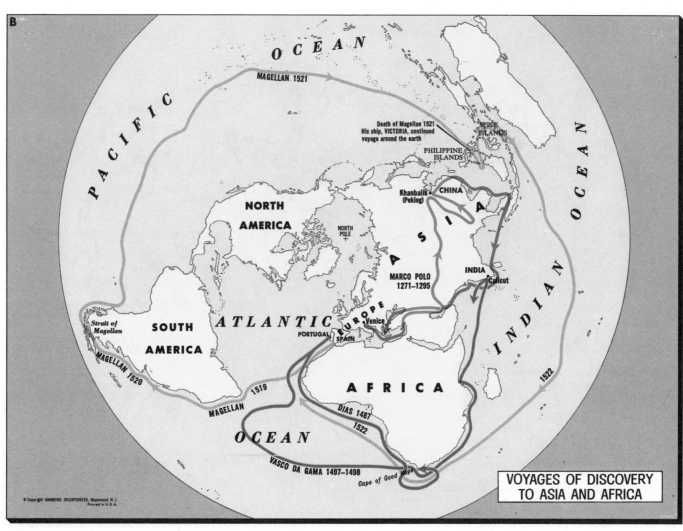

B

VOYAGES OF DISCOVERY TO ASIA AND AFRICA

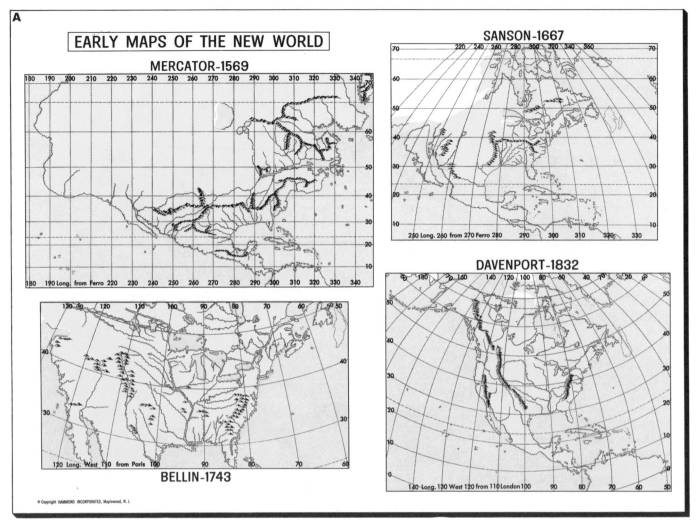

A

EARLY MAPS OF THE NEW WORLD

MERCATOR-1569

SANSON-1667

DAVENPORT-1832

BELLIN-1743

© Copyright HAMMOND INCORPORATED, Maplewood, N. J.

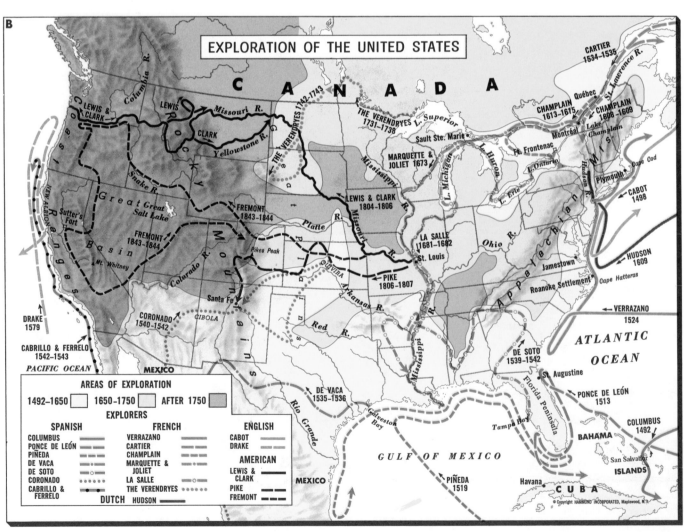

B

EXPLORATION OF THE UNITED STATES

AREAS OF EXPLORATION

1492–1650   1650–1750   AFTER 1750

EXPLORERS

SPANISH	FRENCH	ENGLISH
COLUMBUS	VERRAZANO	CABOT
PONCE DE LEÓN	CARTIER	DRAKE
PIÑEDA	CHAMPLAIN	**AMERICAN**
DE VACA	MARQUETTE & JOLIET	LEWIS & CLARK
DE SOTO	LA SALLE	PIKE
CORONADO	THE VERENDRYES	FREMONT
CABRILLO & FERRELO	**DUTCH** HUDSON	

© Copyright HAMMOND INCORPORATED, Maplewood, N. J.

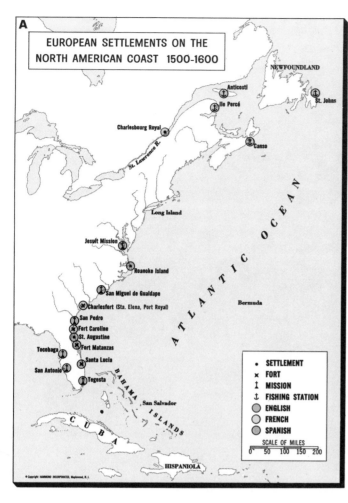

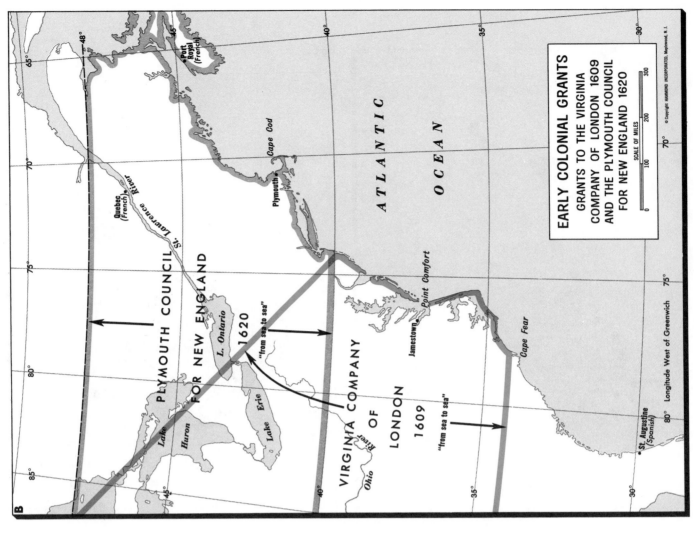

EARLY COLONIAL GRANTS

GRANTS TO THE VIRGINIA
COMPANY OF LONDON 1609
AND THE PLYMOUTH COUNCIL
FOR NEW ENGLAND 1620

SCALE OF MILES

0   100   200   300

© Copyright HAMMOND INCORPORATED, Maplewood, N.J.

PLYMOUTH COUNCIL
FOR NEW ENGLAND
1620

VIRGINIA COMPANY
OF
LONDON
1609

"from sea to sea"

"from sea to sea"

Quebec (French)
Port Royal (French)
St. Lawrence River
Cape Cod
Plymouth
ATLANTIC OCEAN
Lake Huron
Lake Erie
L. Ontario
Ohio River
Jamestown
Point Comfort
Cape Fear
St. Augustine (Spanish)

Longitude West of Greenwich

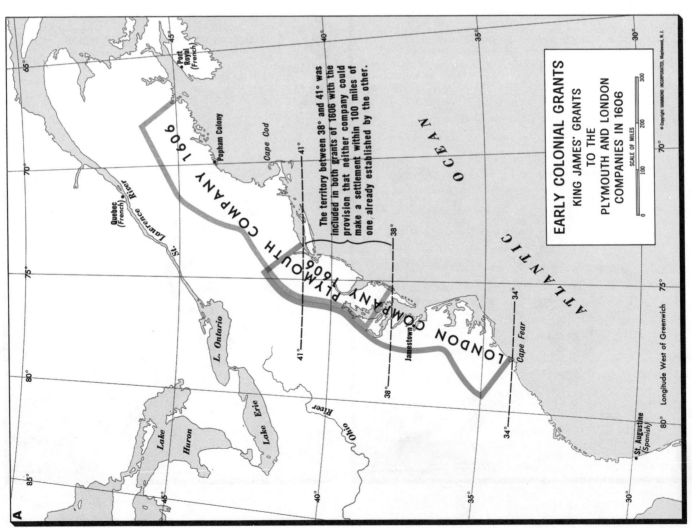

EARLY COLONIAL GRANTS

KING JAMES' GRANTS
TO THE
PLYMOUTH AND LONDON
COMPANIES IN 1606

SCALE OF MILES

0   100   200   300

© Copyright HAMMOND INCORPORATED, Maplewood, N.J.

PLYMOUTH COMPANY 1606

LONDON COMPANY 1606

The territory between 38° and 41° was
included in both grants of 1606 with the
provision that neither company could
make a settlement within 100 miles of
one already established by the other.

Quebec (French)
Port Royal (French)
St. Lawrence River
Popham Colony
Cape Cod
ATLANTIC OCEAN
Lake Huron
Lake Erie
L. Ontario
Ohio River
Jamestown
Cape Fear
St. Augustine (Spanish)

Longitude West of Greenwich

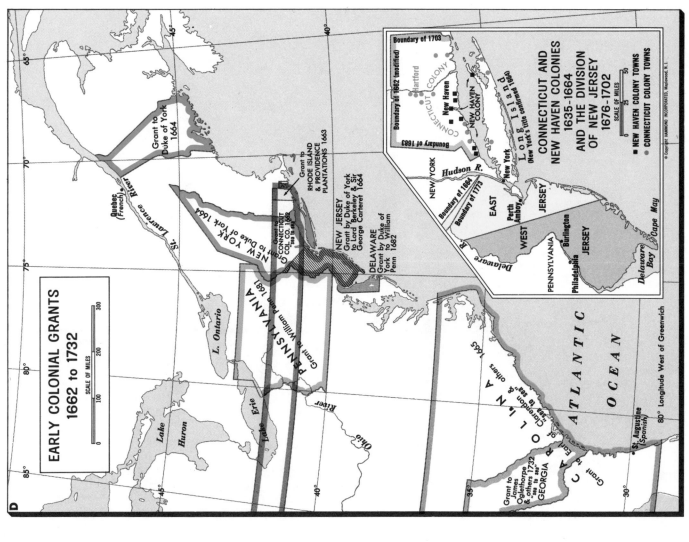

EARLY COLONIAL GRANTS 1662 to 1732

SCALE OF MILES
0   100   200   300

CONNECTICUT AND NEW HAVEN COLONIES 1635-1664 AND THE DIVISION OF NEW JERSEY 1676-1702

SCALE OF MILES
0   25   50

■ NEW HAVEN COLONY TOWNS
● CONNECTICUT COLONY TOWNS

© Copyright HAMMOND INCORPORATED, Maplewood, N.J.

Boundary of 1703
Boundary of 1662 (modified)
Hartford
New Haven
NEW HAVEN COLONY
CONNECTICUT COLONY
Boundary of 1683
New York's title confirmed 1664
Long Island

NEW YORK
Hudson R.
Boundary of 1664
Boundary of 1773
New York
Perth Amboy
EAST JERSEY
WEST JERSEY
PENNSYLVANIA
Philadelphia
Burlington
Delaware Bay
Cape May

Grant to Duke of York 1664
Quebec (French)
St. Lawrence River
L. Ontario
Lake Erie
Lake Huron
Ohio River

NEW YORK
Grant to Duke of York 1664
CONNECTICUT COL. CO. 1662 "sea to sea"
Grant to William Penn 1681
PENNSYLVANIA
Grant to RHODE ISLAND & PROVIDENCE PLANTATIONS 1663
NEW JERSEY Grant by Duke of York to Lord Berkeley & Sir George Carteret 1664
DELAWARE Grant by Duke of York to William Penn 1682

Clarendon "sea to sea" & others 1665
CAROLINA
Grant to Fort "sea to sea"
Grant to James Oglethorpe & others 1732 "sea to sea" GEORGIA
St. Augustine (Spanish)

ATLANTIC OCEAN
80° Longitude West of Greenwich

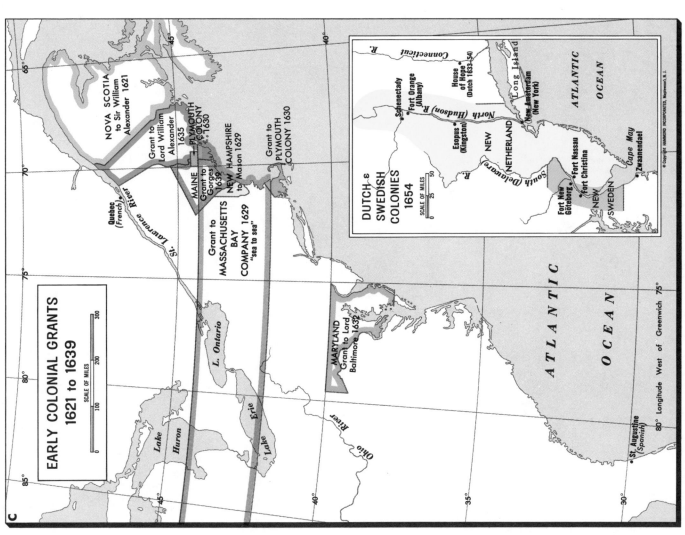

EARLY COLONIAL GRANTS 1621 to 1639

SCALE OF MILES
0   100   200   300

DUTCH & SWEDISH COLONIES 1654

SCALE OF MILES
0   25   50

© Copyright HAMMOND INCORPORATED, Maplewood, R.I.

Connecticut R.
Schenectady
Fort Orange (Albany)
House of Hope (Dutch 1633-54)
Esopus (Kingston)
North (Hudson) R.
NEW NETHERLAND
New Amsterdam (New York)
Long Island
South (Delaware) R.
Fort Nassau
Fort New Göteborg
Fort Christina
NEW SWEDEN
Zwaanendael
Cape May
ATLANTIC OCEAN

Quebec (French)
St. Lawrence River
L. Ontario
Lake Erie
Lake Huron
Ohio River

NOVA SCOTIA to Sir William Alexander 1621
Grant to Lord William Alexander 1635
MAINE Grant to Gorges 1639
PLYMOUTH COLONY 1630
NEW HAMPSHIRE to Mason 1629
Grant to MASSACHUSETTS BAY COMPANY 1629 "sea to sea"
Grant to PLYMOUTH COLONY 1630
MARYLAND Grant to Lord Baltimore 1632

ATLANTIC OCEAN
St. Augustine (Spanish)
80° Longitude West of Greenwich 75°

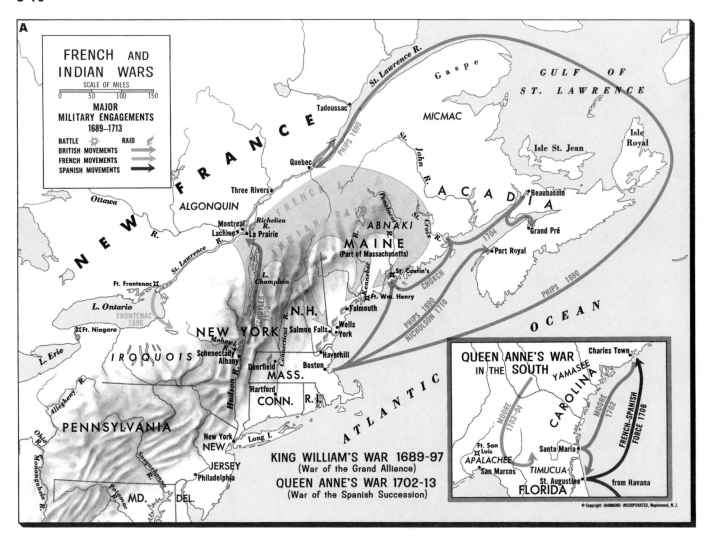

A

FRENCH AND INDIAN WARS

SCALE OF MILES
0 50 100 150

MAJOR MILITARY ENGAGEMENTS 1689–1713

BATTLE ☀ RAID 🖋
BRITISH MOVEMENTS →
FRENCH MOVEMENTS →
SPANISH MOVEMENTS →

KING WILLIAM'S WAR 1689-97
(War of the Grand Alliance)

QUEEN ANNE'S WAR 1702-13
(War of the Spanish Succession)

QUEEN ANNE'S WAR IN THE SOUTH

© Copyright HAMMOND INCORPORATED, Maplewood, N.J.

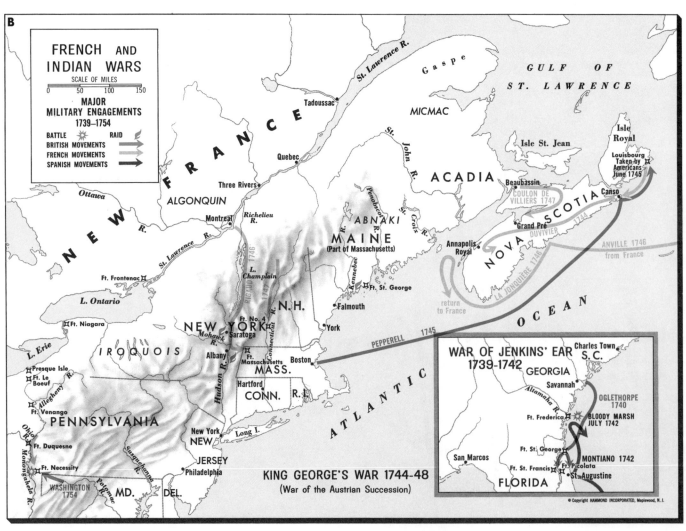

B

FRENCH AND INDIAN WARS

SCALE OF MILES
0 50 100 150

MAJOR MILITARY ENGAGEMENTS 1739–1754

BATTLE ☀ RAID 🖋
BRITISH MOVEMENTS →
FRENCH MOVEMENTS →
SPANISH MOVEMENTS →

KING GEORGE'S WAR 1744-48
(War of the Austrian Succession)

WAR OF JENKINS' EAR 1739-1742

© Copyright HAMMOND INCORPORATED, Maplewood, N.J.

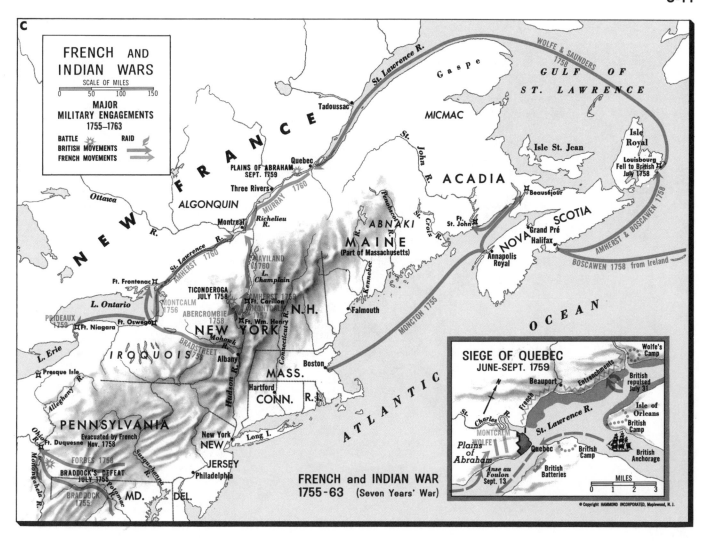

C

FRENCH AND INDIAN WARS

SCALE OF MILES

0   50   100   150

MAJOR MILITARY ENGAGEMENTS 1755–1763

BATTLE ⚔   RAID
BRITISH MOVEMENTS →
FRENCH MOVEMENTS →

FRENCH and INDIAN WAR 1755-63 (Seven Years' War)

SIEGE OF QUEBEC JUNE–SEPT. 1759

© Copyright HAMMOND INCORPORATED, Maplewood, N.J.

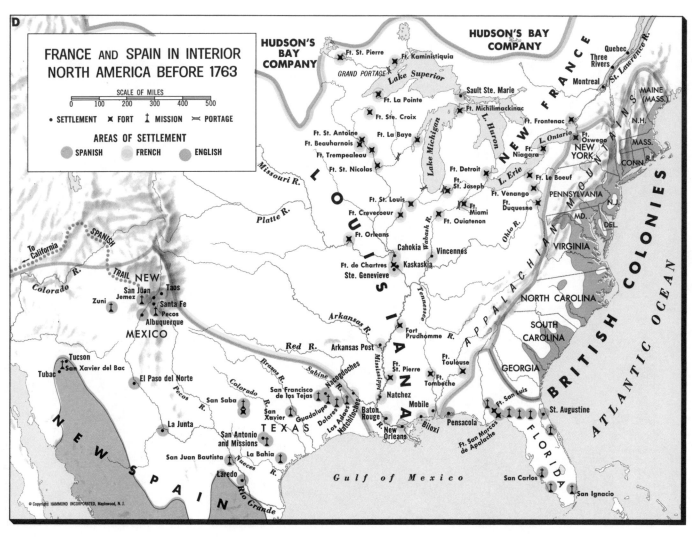

D

FRANCE AND SPAIN IN INTERIOR NORTH AMERICA BEFORE 1763

SCALE OF MILES

0   100   200   300   400   500

● SETTLEMENT   ✕ FORT   ⌘ MISSION   ⋈ PORTAGE

AREAS OF SETTLEMENT

SPANISH   FRENCH   ENGLISH

© Copyright HAMMOND INCORPORATED, Maplewood, N.J.

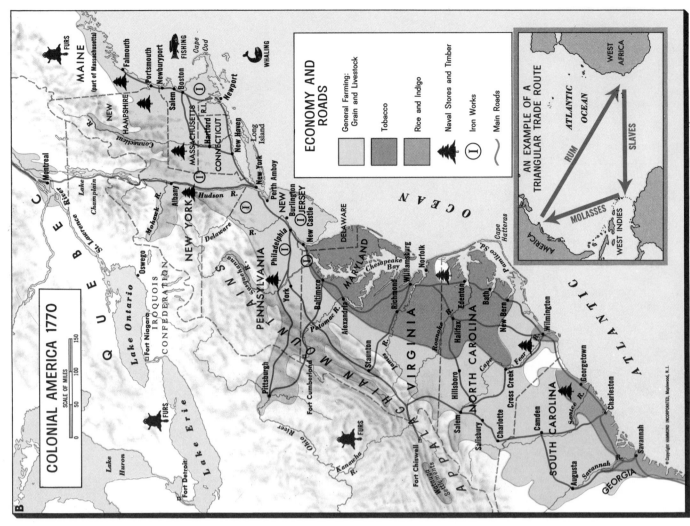

COLONIAL AMERICA 1770

SCALE OF MILES
0 50 100 150

ECONOMY AND ROADS

- General Farming: Grain and Livestock
- Tobacco
- Rice and Indigo
- Naval Stores and Timber
- Iron Works
- Main Roads

AN EXAMPLE OF A TRIANGULAR TRADE ROUTE

WEST AFRICA
ATLANTIC OCEAN
RUM
SLAVES
MOLASSES
AMERICA
WEST INDIES

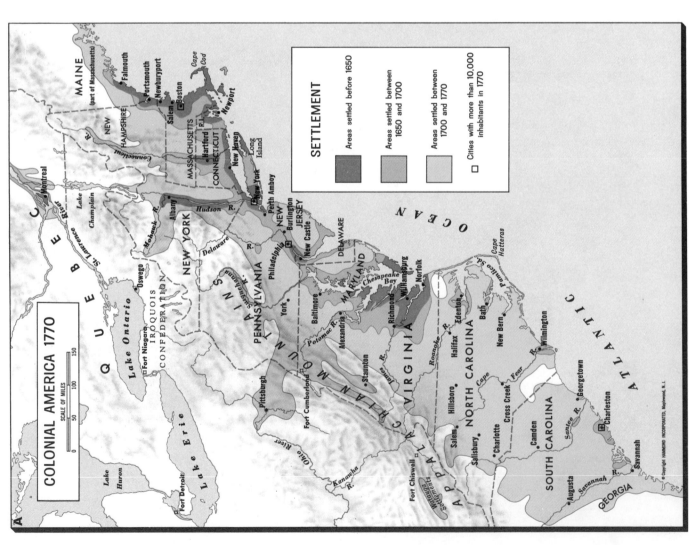

COLONIAL AMERICA 1770

SCALE OF MILES
0 50 100 150

SETTLEMENT

- Areas settled before 1650
- Areas settled between 1650 and 1700
- Areas settled between 1700 and 1770
- Cities with more than 10,000 inhabitants in 1770

© Copyright HAMMOND INCORPORATED, Maplewood, N.J.

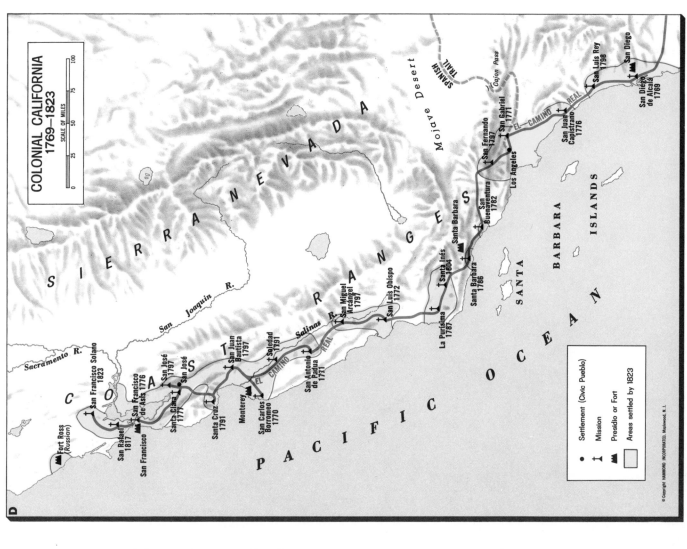

COLONIAL CALIFORNIA 1769–1823

SCALE OF MILES
0 25 50 75 100

Legend
- ● Settlement (Civic Pueblo)
- ⵜ Mission
- ▲ Presidio or Fort
- ▨ Areas settled by 1823

© Copyright HAMMOND INCORPORATED, Maplewood, N.J.

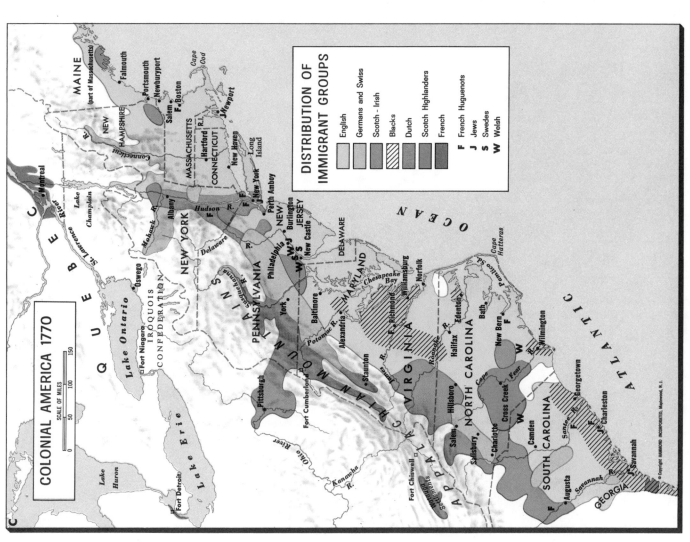

COLONIAL AMERICA 1770

SCALE OF MILES
0 50 100 150

DISTRIBUTION OF IMMIGRANT GROUPS

- English
- Germans and Swiss
- Scotch - Irish
- Blacks
- Dutch
- Scotch Highlanders
- French
- **F** French Huguenots
- **J** Jews
- **S** Swedes
- **W** Welsh

© Copyright HAMMOND INCORPORATED, Maplewood, N.J.

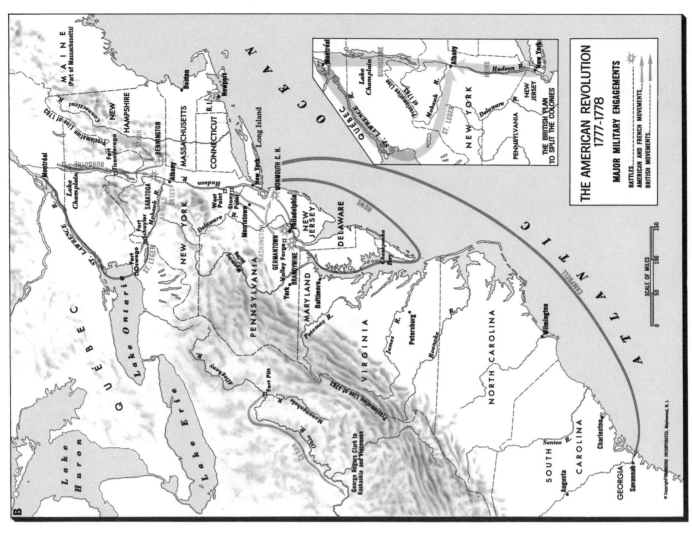

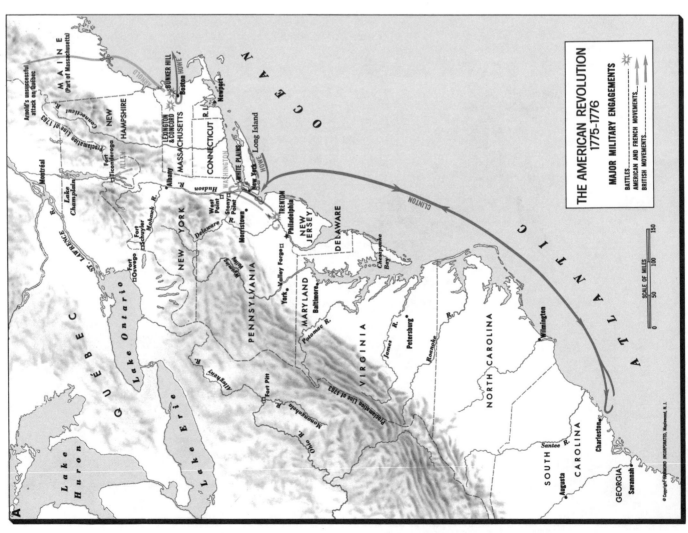

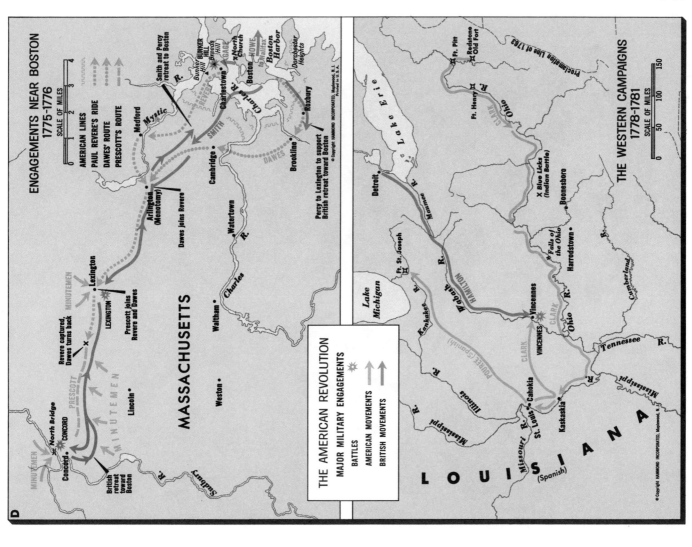

ENGAGEMENTS NEAR BOSTON
1775-1776

SCALE OF MILES

0 1 2 3 4

AMERICAN LINES
PAUL REVERE'S RIDE
DAWES' ROUTE
PRESCOTT'S ROUTE

MASSACHUSETTS

Medford
Arlington (Menotomy)
Dawes joins Revere
Watertown
Charles R.
Waltham
Weston
Lincoln
Lexington
LEXINGTON
Prescott joins Revere and Dawes
MINUTEMEN
Revere captured, Dawes turns back
PRESCOTT
MINUTEMEN
North Bridge CONCORD
Concord
British retreat toward Boston
Sudbury R.

Mystic R.
Charles R.
SMITH
Smith and Percy retreat to Boston
BUNKER HILL
Breeds Hill
North Church
Charlestown
HOWE, to Halifax
Boston
Boston Harbor
Cambridge
DAWES
GAGE
Dorchester Heights
Roxbury
Brookline
Percy to Lexington to support British retreat toward Boston

© Copyright HAMMOND INCORPORATED, Maplewood, N.J. Printed in U.S.A.

THE WESTERN CAMPAIGNS
1778-1781

SCALE OF MILES

0 50 100 150

Lake Erie
Detroit
Ft. Pitt
Redstone Old Fort
Ft. Henry
Ohio R.
Proclamation Line of 1763
CLARK
Maumee R.
HAMILTON
Lake Michigan
Ft. St. Joseph
Wabash R.
Kaskaskia R.
CLARK
Vincennes
VINCENNES
X Blue Licks (Indian Battle)
Boonesboro
Harrodstown
Falls of the Ohio
Ohio R.
Cumberland R.
Tennessee R.
Missouri R.
St. Louis
Cahokia
Kaskaskia
POUREE (Spanish)
Illinois R.
Mississippi R.
Mississippi R.
LOUISIANA
(Spanish)

THE AMERICAN REVOLUTION
MAJOR MILITARY ENGAGEMENTS
BATTLES
AMERICAN MOVEMENTS
BRITISH MOVEMENTS

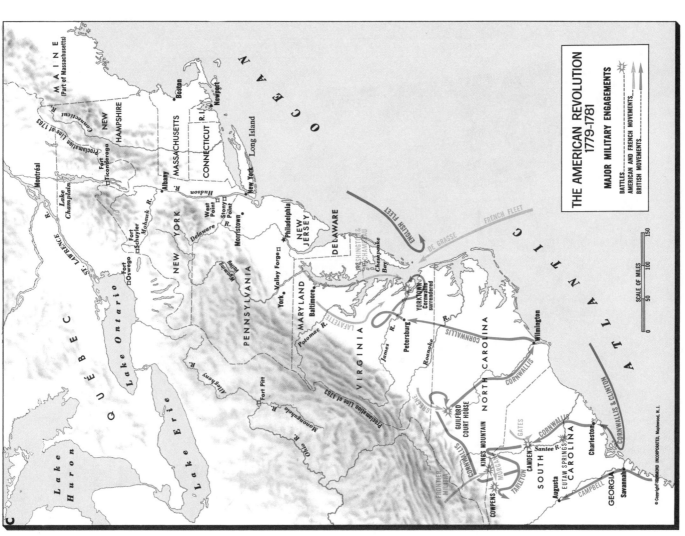

THE AMERICAN REVOLUTION
1779-1781

MAJOR MILITARY ENGAGEMENTS
BATTLES
AMERICAN AND FRENCH MOVEMENTS
BRITISH MOVEMENTS

SCALE OF MILES

0 50 100 150

Lake Huron
Lake Erie
Lake Ontario
QUEBEC
Montréal
Lake Champlain
Fort Ticonderoga
Connecticut R.
MAINE (Part of Massachusetts)
NEW HAMPSHIRE
MASSACHUSETTS
Boston
R.I.
Newport
CONNECTICUT
Albany
Fort Schuyler
Mohawk R.
Fort Oswego
St. Lawrence R.
Hudson R.
West Point
Stony Point
NEW YORK
Long Island
New York
NEW JERSEY
Morristown
Wyoming Valley
PENNSYLVANIA
Allegheny R.
Fort Pitt
Monongahela R.
Ohio R.
Proclamation Line of 1763
Valley Forge
York
Philadelphia
DELAWARE
MARYLAND
Baltimore
Potomac R.
VIRGINIA
James R.
Petersburg
Roanoke R.
LAFAYETTE
CORNWALLIS
YORKTOWN Cornwallis surrendered
Chesapeake Bay
WASHINGTON & ROCHAMBEAU
ENGLISH FLEET
DE GRASSE
FRENCH FLEET
ATLANTIC OCEAN
NORTH CAROLINA
Wilmington
GUILFORD COURT HOUSE
GREENE
CORNWALLIS
KINGS MOUNTAIN
MORGAN
GATES
SOUTH CAROLINA
Santee R.
FRONTIER MILITIA
TARLETON
CAMDEN
EUTAW SPRINGS
COWPENS
Augusta
Charleston
CORNWALLIS & CLINTON
GEORGIA
Savannah
CAMPBELL

© Copyright HAMMOND INCORPORATED, Maplewood, N.J.

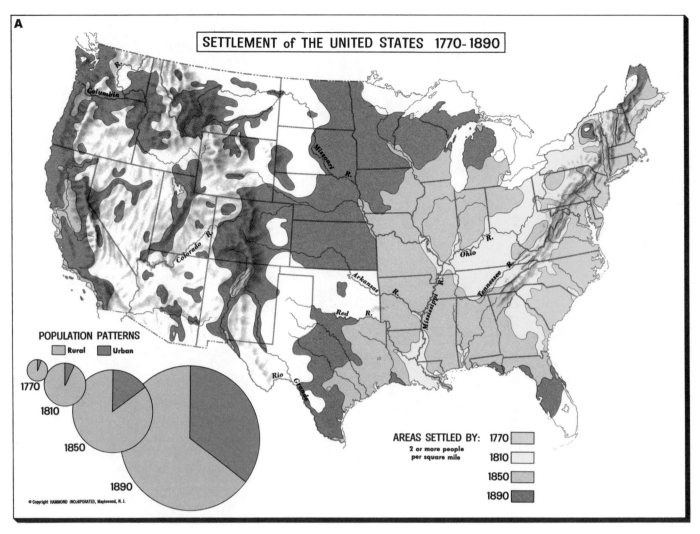

A

SETTLEMENT of THE UNITED STATES 1770-1890

POPULATION PATTERNS

Rural Urban

1770
1810
1850
1890

© Copyright HAMMOND INCORPORATED, Maplewood, N.J.

AREAS SETTLED BY: 1770
2 or more people per square mile
1810
1850
1890

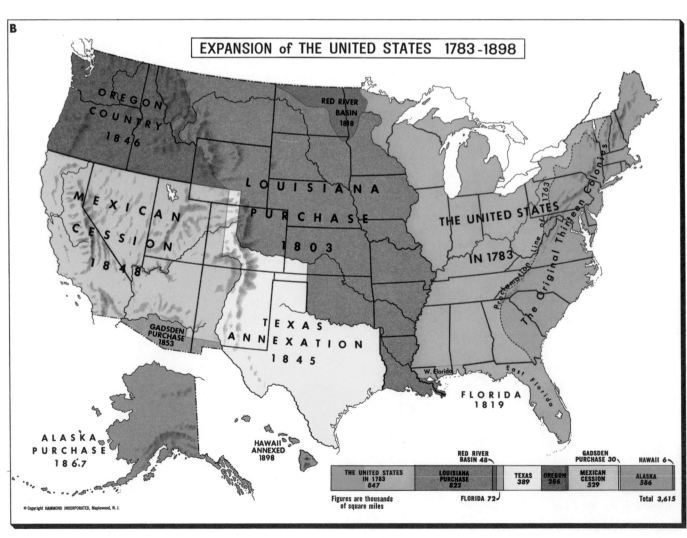

B

EXPANSION of THE UNITED STATES 1783-1898

OREGON COUNTRY 1846

RED RIVER BASIN 1818

MEXICAN CESSION 1848

LOUISIANA PURCHASE 1803

THE UNITED STATES IN 1783

Proclamation Line of 1763

The Original Thirteen Colonies

GADSDEN PURCHASE 1853

TEXAS ANNEXATION 1845

W. Florida

East Florida

FLORIDA 1819

ALASKA PURCHASE 1867

HAWAII ANNEXED 1898

© Copyright HAMMOND INCORPORATED, Maplewood, N.J.

THE UNITED STATES IN 1783 847	LOUISIANA PURCHASE 822	TEXAS 389	OREGON 286	MEXICAN CESSION 529	ALASKA 586

RED RIVER BASIN 48
GADSDEN PURCHASE 30
HAWAII 6

Figures are thousands of square miles

FLORIDA 72

Total 3,615

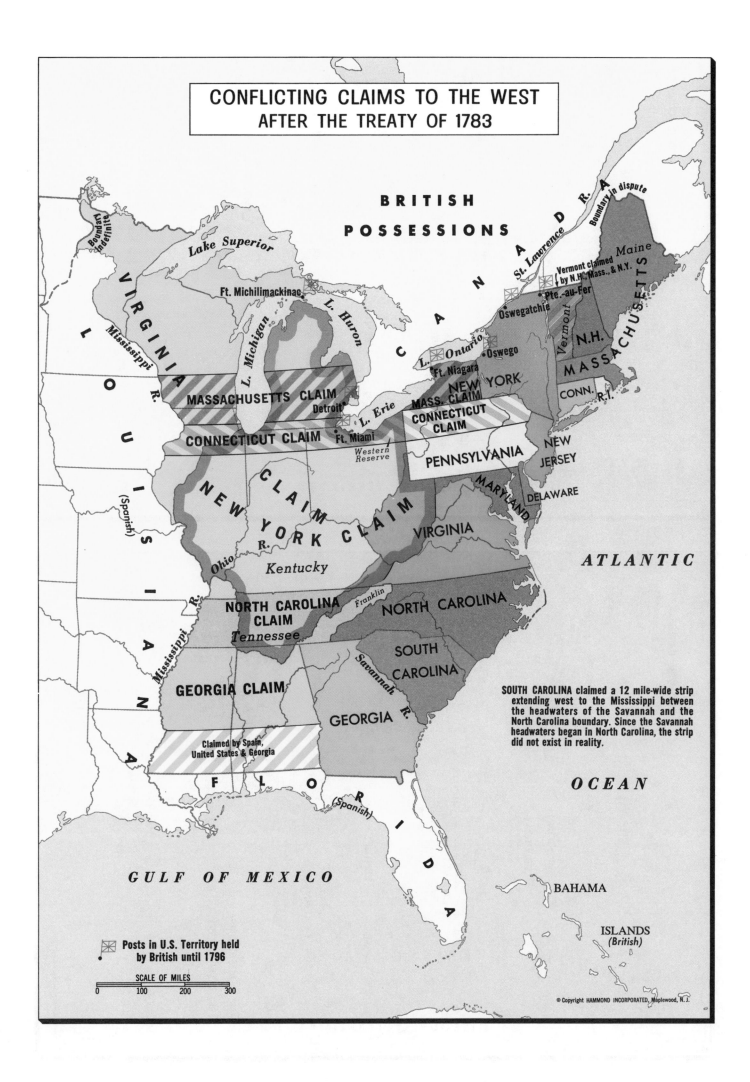

CONFLICTING CLAIMS TO THE WEST AFTER THE TREATY OF 1783

BRITISH POSSESSIONS

CANADA

Lake Superior

Ft. Michilimackinac

L. Huron

L. Michigan

LOUISIANA

VIRGINIA

MASSACHUSETTS CLAIM

Detroit

CONNECTICUT CLAIM

Ft. Miami

Western Reserve

NEW YORK CLAIM

CLAIM

Ohio R.

Kentucky

Mississippi R.

(Spanish)

NORTH CAROLINA CLAIM

Tennessee

Franklin

GEORGIA CLAIM

Mississippi R.

Claimed by Spain, United States & Georgia

FLORIDA

(Spanish)

St. Lawrence R.

Boundary in dispute

Vermont claimed by N.H., Mass., & N.Y.

Maine

Pte.-au-Fer

Oswegatchie

N.H.

L. Ontario

Oswego

Ft. Niagara

L. Erie

MASSACHUSETTS

Vermont

NEW YORK

MASS. CLAIM

CONNECTICUT CLAIM

CONN.

R.I.

PENNSYLVANIA

NEW JERSEY

MARYLAND

DELAWARE

VIRGINIA

NORTH CAROLINA

SOUTH CAROLINA

Savannah R.

GEORGIA

ATLANTIC

OCEAN

SOUTH CAROLINA claimed a 12 mile-wide strip extending west to the Mississippi between the headwaters of the Savannah and the North Carolina boundary. Since the Savannah headwaters began in North Carolina, the strip did not exist in reality.

Boundary indefinite

GULF OF MEXICO

BAHAMA

ISLANDS
(British)

⊠ Posts in U.S. Territory held
  • by British until 1796

SCALE OF MILES

0   100   200   300

© Copyright HAMMOND INCORPORATED, Maplewood, N. J.

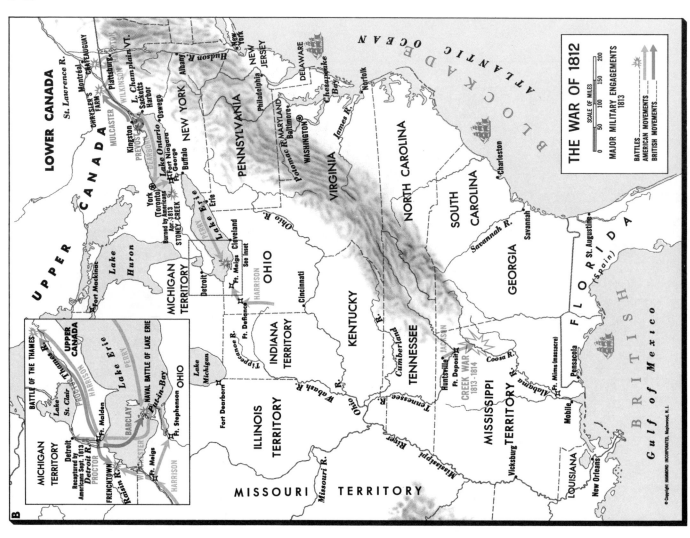

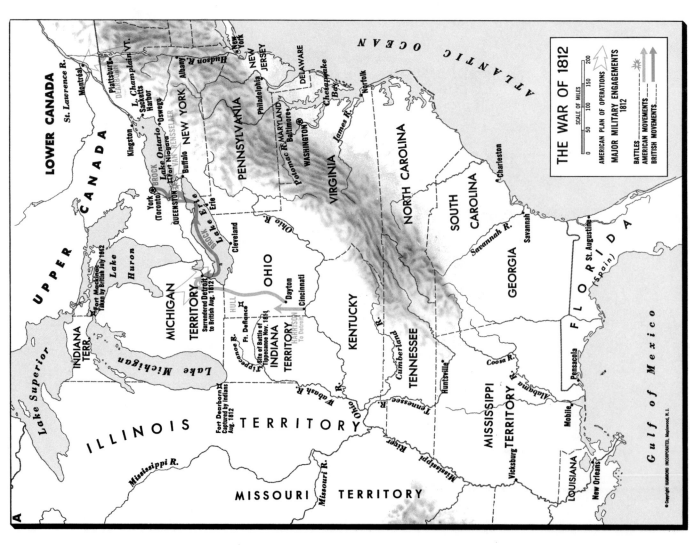

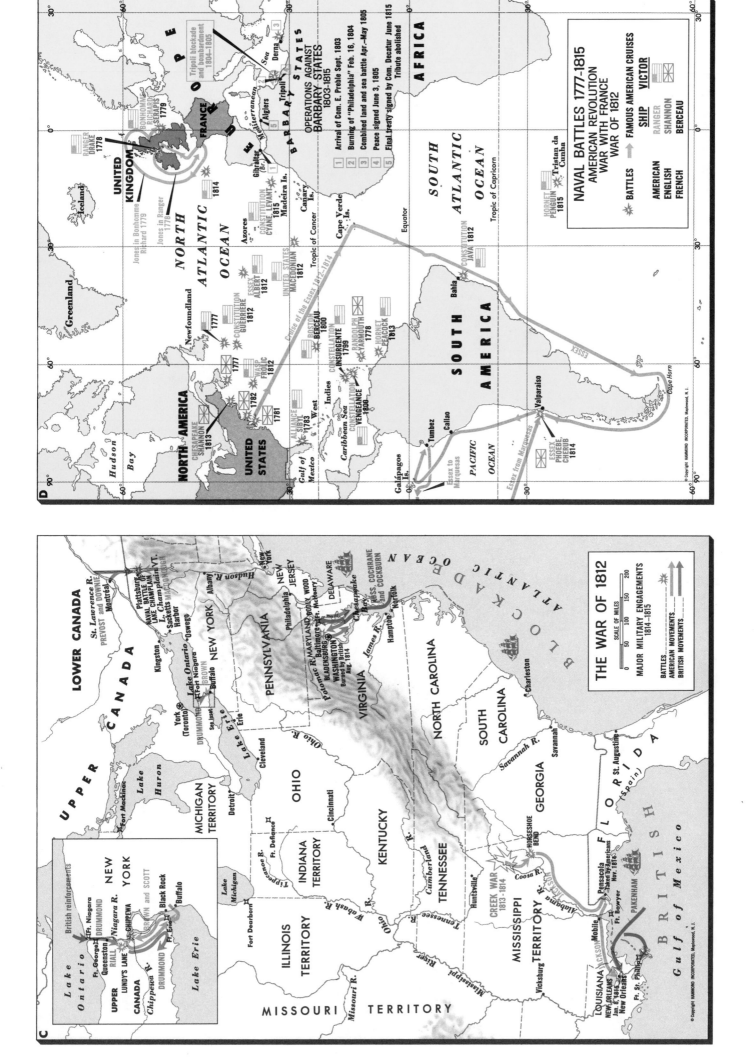

D

NAVAL BATTLES 1777–1815
AMERICAN REVOLUTION
WAR WITH FRANCE
WAR OF 1812

Greenland

Iceland

NORTH ATLANTIC OCEAN

EUROPE

UNITED KINGDOM

Jones in Bonhomme Richard 1779
Jones in Ranger 1778

BONHOMME RICHARD SERAPIS 1779
RANGER DRAKE 1778

FRANCE

Mediterranean Sea

Tripoli blockade and bombardment 1804–1805

BARBARY STATES

Gibraltar (Br.)
Algiers
Tripoli
Derna

OPERATIONS AGAINST BARBARY STATES 1803–1815

1 Arrival of Com. E. Preble Sept. 1803
2 Burning of "Philadelphia" Feb. 16, 1804
3 Combined land and sea battle Apr.–May 1805
4 Peace signed June 3, 1805
5 Final treaty signed by Com. Decatur June 1815 Tribute abolished

AFRICA

Madeira Is.
Canary Is.
Cape Verde Is.

Tropic of Cancer

1814

CONSTITUTION CYANE LEVANT 1815

Azores

Newfoundland

1777
1777
1781
1782

CONSTITUTION GUERRIÈRE 1812

ESSEX ALBERT 1812

UNITED STATES MACEDONIAN 1812

WASP FROLIC 1812

CHESAPEAKE SHANNON 1813

NORTH AMERICA

UNITED STATES

Hudson Bay

ALLIANCE SIBYL 1783

Gulf of Mexico

West Indies

Caribbean Sea

CONSTELLATION INSURGENTE 1799

CONSTELLATION VENGEANCE 1800

BOSTON BERCEAU 1800

RANDOLPH YARMOUTH 1778

HORNET PEACOCK 1813

Cruise of the Essex 1812–1814

Tropic of Cancer

Equator

SOUTH AMERICA

Bahia

CONSTITUTION JAVA 1812

Galápagos Is.

Essex to Marquesas

Tumbez
Callao

Essex from Marquesas

PACIFIC OCEAN

Valparaíso

ESSEX PHOEBE, CHERUB 1814

Cape Horn

SOUTH ATLANTIC OCEAN

Tropic of Capricorn

HORNET PENGUIN 1815
Tristan da Cunha

NAVAL BATTLES 1777–1815
AMERICAN REVOLUTION
WAR WITH FRANCE
WAR OF 1812

SHIP   VICTOR
RANGER
SHANNON
BERCEAU

BATTLES   FAMOUS AMERICAN CRUISES

AMERICAN
ENGLISH
FRENCH

© Copyright HAMMOND INCORPORATED, Maplewood, N.J.

C

LOWER CANADA

St. Lawrence R.
PREVOST and DOWNIE
Montréal

Plattsburg
NAVAL BATTLE OF LAKE CHAMPLAIN
L. Champlain Vt.
Sackett's Harbor
Oswego
Kingston

UPPER CANADA

Lake Huron
Fort Mackinac

York (Toronto)
DRUMMOND
Sea Iset

Lake Ontario
BROWN
Fort Niagara
Buffalo

Lake Erie
Lake Erie

Fort Dearborn

MICHIGAN TERRITORY

Detroit

Ft. Defiance

ILLINOIS TERRITORY

INDIANA TERRITORY

Tippecanoe R.
Wabash R.

OHIO

Cleveland
Cincinnati
Ohio R.

MISSOURI TERRITORY

Missouri R.
Mississippi River

KENTUCKY

Cumberland R.
Tennessee R.

TENNESSEE

Huntsville

Nashville

Vicksburg

MISSISSIPPI TERRITORY

Mobile
Pensacola

CREEK WAR 1813–1814
HORSESHOE BEND
Coosa R.
Alabama R.

Jackson

LOUISIANA
NEW ORLEANS Jan. 8, 1815
New Orleans
Ft. St. Philip

PAKENHAM

Ft. Bowyer

BRITISH FLORIDA (Spain)

St. Augustine

Gulf of Mexico

GEORGIA

Savannah R.

SOUTH CAROLINA

Charleston

NORTH CAROLINA

VIRGINIA

James R.
Hampton
Norfolk

ROSS, COCHRANE and COCKBURN

Chesapeake Bay

DELAWARE

MARYLAND
Baltimore
WASHINGTON Burned by British Aug. 1814
BLADENSBURG
Potomac R.
Fort McHenry

PENNSYLVANIA

Philadelphia

NEW JERSEY

New York

Albany
Hudson R.

NEW YORK

ATLANTIC OCEAN

BLOCKADE

THE WAR OF 1812

SCALE OF MILES
0 50 100 150 200

MAJOR MILITARY ENGAGEMENTS 1814–1815

BATTLES
AMERICAN MOVEMENTS
BRITISH MOVEMENTS

Lake Ontario
Ft. George
Queenston
UPPER CANADA
Chippewa R.
LUNDY'S LANE
DRUMMOND

Ft. Niagara
British reinforcements
DRUMMOND
RIALL
CHIPPEWA
BROWN and SCOTT

NEW YORK

Black Rock
Buffalo
Ft. Erie
Lake Erie

Pensacola Taken by Americans Nov. 1814

© Copyright HAMMOND INCORPORATED, Maplewood, N.J.

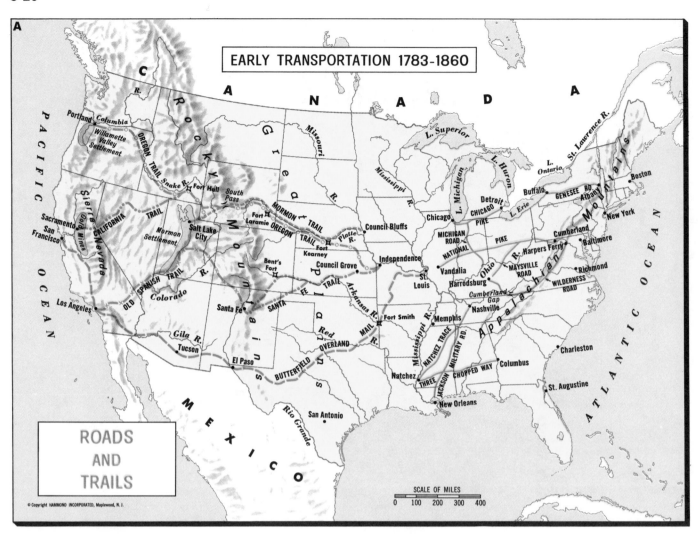

EARLY TRANSPORTATION 1783-1860

ROADS AND TRAILS

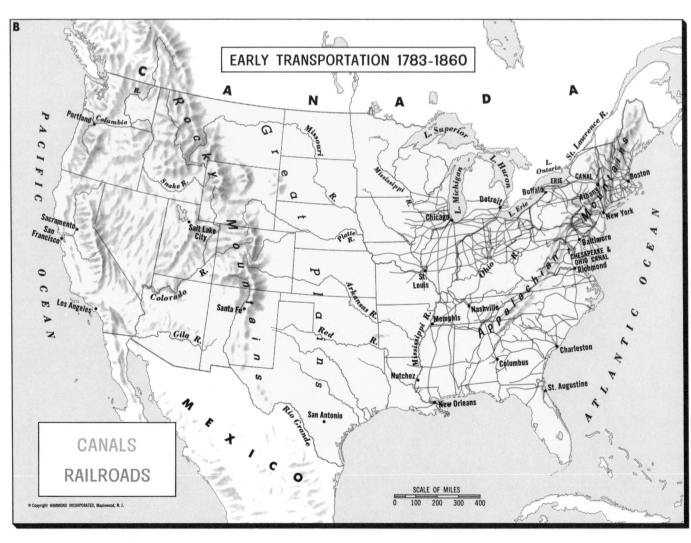

EARLY TRANSPORTATION 1783-1860

CANALS RAILROADS

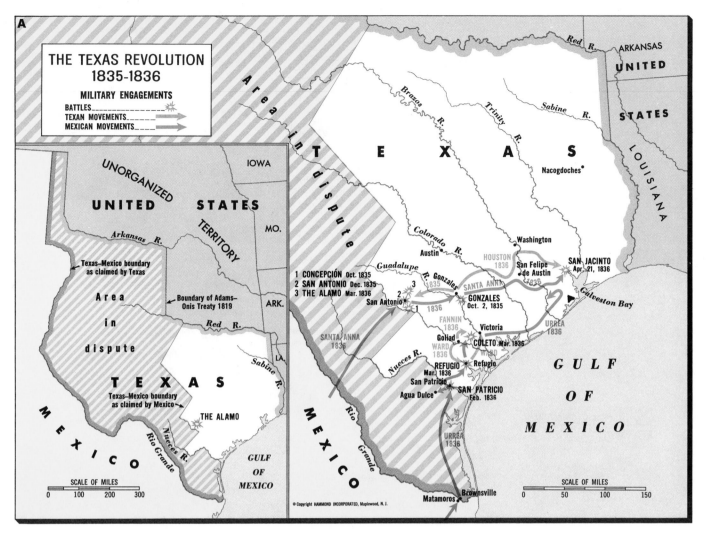

A

THE TEXAS REVOLUTION
1835-1836
MILITARY ENGAGEMENTS
BATTLES
TEXAN MOVEMENTS
MEXICAN MOVEMENTS

UNORGANIZED

UNITED **STATES**
TERRITORY

IOWA

MO.

Arkansas R.

Texas–Mexico boundary
as claimed by Texas

Boundary of Adams–
Onis Treaty 1819

ARK.

A r e a

i n

Red R.

d i s p u t e

Sabine R.

LA.

T E X A S

Texas–Mexico boundary
as claimed by Mexico

THE ALAMO

M E X I C O

Rio Grande

Nueces R.

GULF
OF
MEXICO

SCALE OF MILES
0   100   200   300

T E X A S

Red R.

ARKANSAS

UNITED

Brazos R.

Trinity R.

Sabine R.

S T A T E S

Nacogdoches

LOUISIANA

A r e a   i n   d i s p u t e

Colorado R.

Washington

Guadalupe R.

Austin

HOUSTON
1836

San Felipe
de Austin

SAN JACINTO
Apr. 21, 1836

1 CONCEPCIÓN Oct. 1835
2 SAN ANTONIO Dec. 1835
3 THE ALAMO Mar. 1836

SANTA ANNA

Gonzales

3

2   1

San Antonio

GONZALES
Oct. 2, 1835

Galveston Bay

FANNIN
1836

SANTA ANNA
1836

Victoria

URREA
1836

Goliad   COLETO Mar. 1836

WARD
1836

WARD

Nueces R.

REFUGIO
Mar. 1836   Refugio

San Patricio

Agua Dulce   SAN PATRICIO
Feb. 1836

GULF

OF

MEXICO

M E X I C O

Rio Grande

URREA
1836

Matamoros   Brownsville

© Copyright HAMMOND INCORPORATED, Maplewood, N.J.

SCALE OF MILES
0   50   100   150

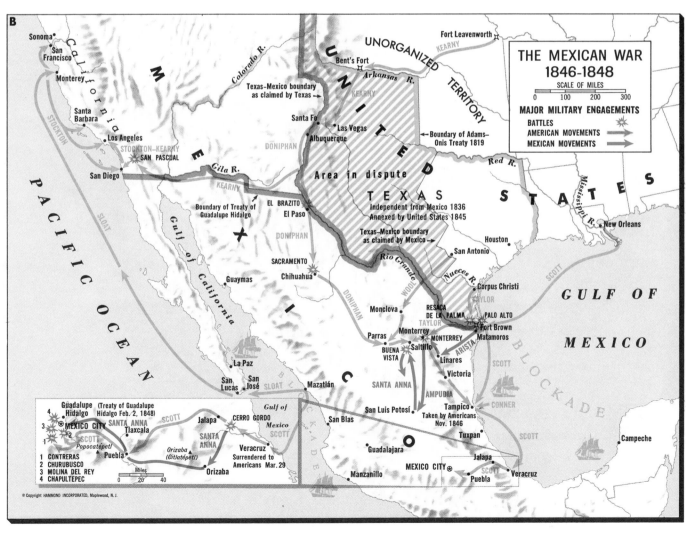

B

Sonoma

San
Francisco   *California*

Monterey

M

Santa
Barbara

Los Angeles

STOCKTON–KEARNY

SAN PASCAL

STOCKTON

San Diego

Gila R.

Colorado R.

UNORGANIZED

Fort Leavenworth

KEARNY

Bent's Fort

Arkansas R.

Texas–Mexico boundary
as claimed by Texas

KEARNY

Santa Fe

Las Vegas

Albuquerque

DONIPHAN

TERRITORY

Boundary of Adams–
Onis Treaty 1819

Red R.

UNITED

THE MEXICAN WAR
1846-1848
SCALE OF MILES
0   100   200   300
MAJOR MILITARY ENGAGEMENTS
BATTLES
AMERICAN MOVEMENTS
MEXICAN MOVEMENTS

A r e a   i n   d i s p u t e

T E X A S

Independent from Mexico 1836
Annexed by United States 1845

S T A T E S

Mississippi R.

New Orleans

E

Boundary of Treaty of
Guadalupe Hidalgo

EL BRAZITO

El Paso

KEARNY

DONIPHAN

SACRAMENTO

Chihuahua

Texas–Mexico boundary
as claimed by Mexico

Rio Grande

Houston

San Antonio

Nueces R.

Corpus Christi

WOOL

SCOTT

GULF   OF

Gulf of California

Guaymas

I

DONIPHAN

Monclova

Parras

Monterrey

RESACA
DE LA PALMA

TAYLOR

MONTERREY   Matamoros

PALO ALTO

Fort Brown

ARISTA

P A C I F I C   O C E A N

SLOAT

La Paz

San
Lucas   San
José

SLOAT

Mazatlán

BUENA
VISTA   Saltillo

Linares

Victoria

SCOTT

BLOCKADE

MEXICO

C

SANTA ANNA

AMPUDIA

San Luis Potosí

SCOTT

CONNER

Guadalupe   (Treaty of Guadalupe
Hidalgo   Hidalgo Feb. 2, 1848)

SANTA ANNA

4

3   MEXICO CITY

2

SCOTT

Popocatépetl

1   CONTRERAS
2   CHURUBUSCO
3   MOLINA DEL REY
4   CHAPULTEPEC

*Orizaba
(Citlatépetl)*

Tlaxcala

Puebla

Orizaba

Jalapa   CERRO GORDO

SANTA ANNA

Veracruz
Surrendered to
Americans Mar. 29

*Gulf of
Mexico*

SCOTT

San Blas

Tampico
Taken by Americans
Nov. 1846

Tuxpan

Guadalajara

O

Campeche

Miles
0   20   40

Manzanillo   MEXICO CITY

Puebla   Veracruz

Jalapa

© Copyright HAMMOND INCORPORATED, Maplewood, N.J.

FREE AND SLAVE AREAS 1821

1. Free by Missouri Compromise—1820

Free by Northwest Ordinance—1787

MAINE 1820

VT. N.H.

NEW YORK MASS. CONN. R.I.

PENNSYLVANIA

N.J.

ILLINOIS INDIANA OHIO

MD. DEL.

MISSOURI 1821

KENTUCKY

VIRGINIA

36° 30'

TERRITORY OF ARKANSAS

TENNESSEE

NORTH CAROLINA

SOUTH CAROLINA

MISSISSIPPI ALABAMA GEORGIA

LOUISIANA

FREE STATES AND TERRITORIES

SLAVE STATES AND TERRITORIES

© Copyright HAMMOND INCORPORATED, Maplewood, N.J.

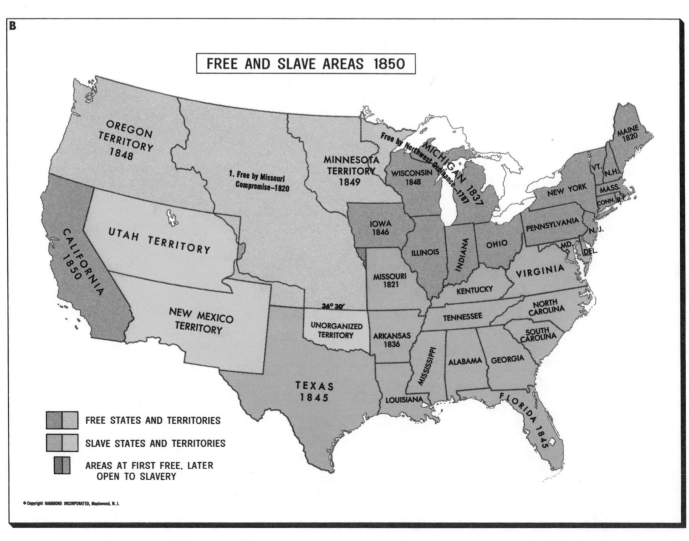

FREE AND SLAVE AREAS 1850

OREGON TERRITORY 1848

1. Free by Missouri Compromise—1820

MINNESOTA TERRITORY 1849

Free by Northwest Ordinance—1787

MICHIGAN 1837

WISCONSIN 1848

MAINE 1820

VT. N.H.

NEW YORK MASS. CONN. R.I.

UTAH TERRITORY

CALIFORNIA 1850

IOWA 1846

ILLINOIS INDIANA OHIO

PENNSYLVANIA

N.J.

MD. DEL.

MISSOURI 1821

KENTUCKY

VIRGINIA

NEW MEXICO TERRITORY

36° 30'

UNORGANIZED TERRITORY

ARKANSAS 1836

TENNESSEE

NORTH CAROLINA

SOUTH CAROLINA

MISSISSIPPI ALABAMA GEORGIA

TEXAS 1845

LOUISIANA

FLORIDA 1845

FREE STATES AND TERRITORIES

SLAVE STATES AND TERRITORIES

AREAS AT FIRST FREE, LATER OPEN TO SLAVERY

© Copyright HAMMOND INCORPORATED, Maplewood, N.J.

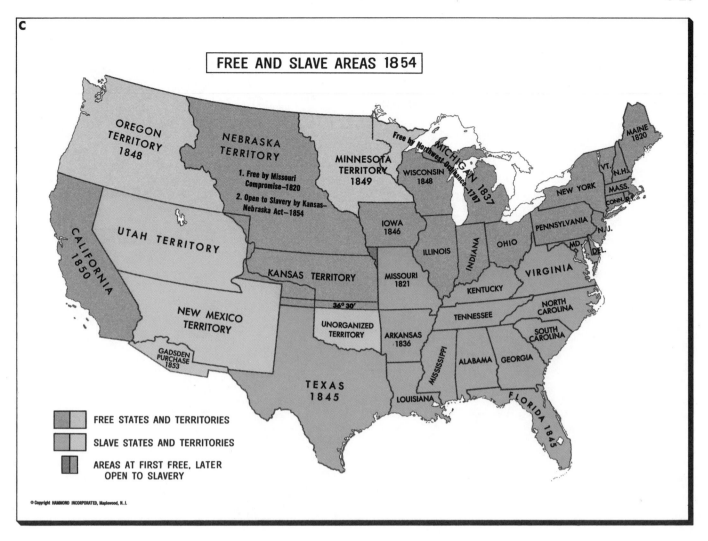

FREE AND SLAVE AREAS 1854

OREGON TERRITORY 1848

NEBRASKA TERRITORY

1. Free by Missouri Compromise—1820
2. Open to Slavery by Kansas–Nebraska Act—1854

MINNESOTA TERRITORY 1849

Free by Northwest Ordinance—1787

MICHIGAN 1837

WISCONSIN 1848

MAINE 1820

UTAH TERRITORY

CALIFORNIA 1850

IOWA 1846

ILLINOIS

INDIANA

OHIO

NEW YORK

PENNSYLVANIA

VT. N.H. MASS. CONN. R.I.

N.J.

MD. DEL.

KANSAS TERRITORY

MISSOURI 1821

VIRGINIA

NEW MEXICO TERRITORY

36° 30'

KENTUCKY

GADSDEN PURCHASE 1853

UNORGANIZED TERRITORY

ARKANSAS 1836

TENNESSEE

NORTH CAROLINA

SOUTH CAROLINA

TEXAS 1845

MISSISSIPPI

ALABAMA

GEORGIA

LOUISIANA

FLORIDA 1845

☐☐ FREE STATES AND TERRITORIES

☐☐ SLAVE STATES AND TERRITORIES

■ AREAS AT FIRST FREE, LATER OPEN TO SLAVERY

© Copyright HAMMOND INCORPORATED, Maplewood, N.J.

FREE AND SLAVE AREAS 1861
at the outbreak of the Civil War

WASHINGTON TERRITORY

OREGON 1859

DAKOTA TERRITORY

MINNESOTA 1858

MICHIGAN

MAINE

NEVADA TERRITORY

UTAH TERRITORY

COLORADO TERRITORY

NEBRASKA TERRITORY

WISCONSIN

IOWA

NEW YORK

VT. N.H. MASS. CONN. R.I.

CALIFORNIA

KANSAS 1861

ILLINOIS

INDIANA

OHIO

PENNSYLVANIA

MASON-DIXON LINE

MD. DEL.

N.J.

PUBLIC LAND

MISSOURI

VIRGINIA

KENTUCKY

NEW MEXICO TERRITORY

INDIAN TERRITORY

ARKANSAS

TENNESSEE

NORTH CAROLINA

SOUTH CAROLINA

TEXAS

MISSISSIPPI

ALABAMA

GEORGIA

LOUISIANA

FLORIDA

■ FREE STATES

■ SLAVE STATES

☐ TERRITORIES OPEN TO SLAVERY BY DRED SCOTT DECISION 1857

© Copyright HAMMOND INCORPORATED, Maplewood, N.J.

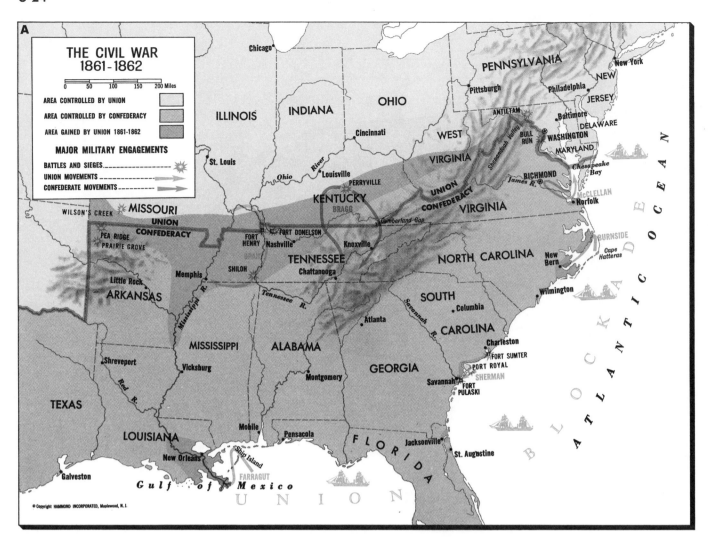

A

THE CIVIL WAR
1861-1862

0   50   100   150   200 Miles

AREA CONTROLLED BY UNION
AREA CONTROLLED BY CONFEDERACY
AREA GAINED BY UNION 1861-1862

MAJOR MILITARY ENGAGEMENTS

BATTLES AND SIEGES
UNION MOVEMENTS
CONFEDERATE MOVEMENTS

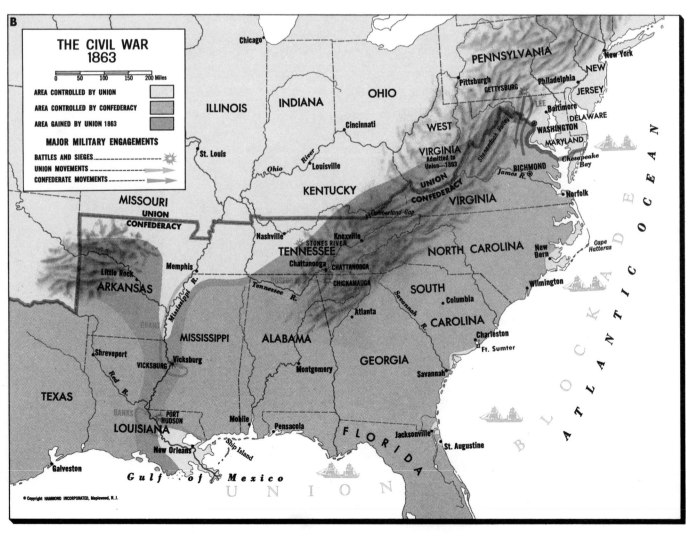

B

THE CIVIL WAR
1863

0   50   100   150   200 Miles

AREA CONTROLLED BY UNION
AREA CONTROLLED BY CONFEDERACY
AREA GAINED BY UNION 1863

MAJOR MILITARY ENGAGEMENTS

BATTLES AND SIEGES
UNION MOVEMENTS
CONFEDERATE MOVEMENTS

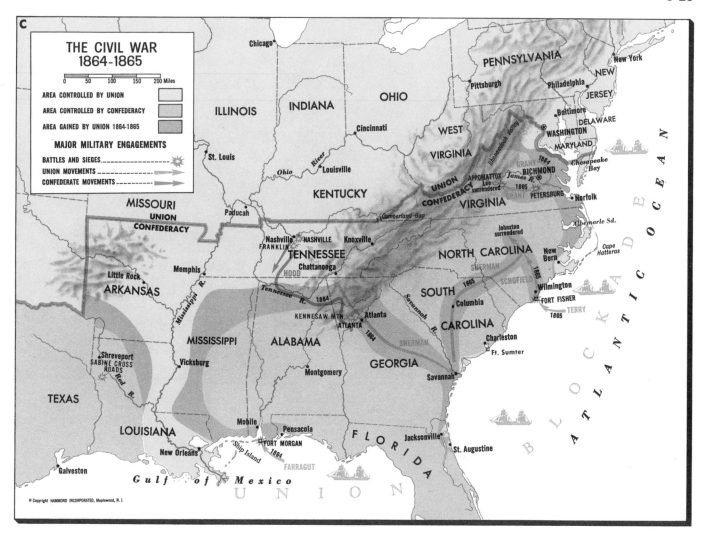

THE CIVIL WAR 1864-1865

0 50 100 150 200 Miles

AREA CONTROLLED BY UNION

AREA CONTROLLED BY CONFEDERACY

AREA GAINED BY UNION 1864-1865

MAJOR MILITARY ENGAGEMENTS

BATTLES AND SIEGES

UNION MOVEMENTS

CONFEDERATE MOVEMENTS

© Copyright HAMMOND INCORPORATED, Maplewood, N.J.

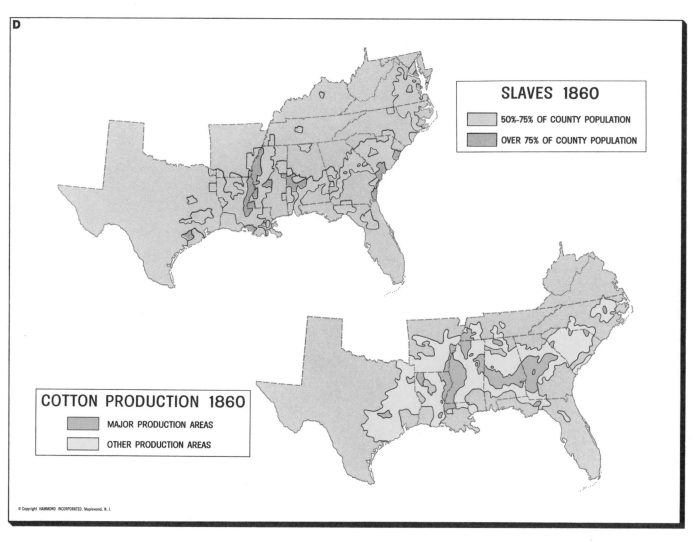

SLAVES 1860

50%-75% OF COUNTY POPULATION

OVER 75% OF COUNTY POPULATION

COTTON PRODUCTION 1860

MAJOR PRODUCTION AREAS

OTHER PRODUCTION AREAS

© Copyright HAMMOND INCORPORATED, Maplewood, N.J.

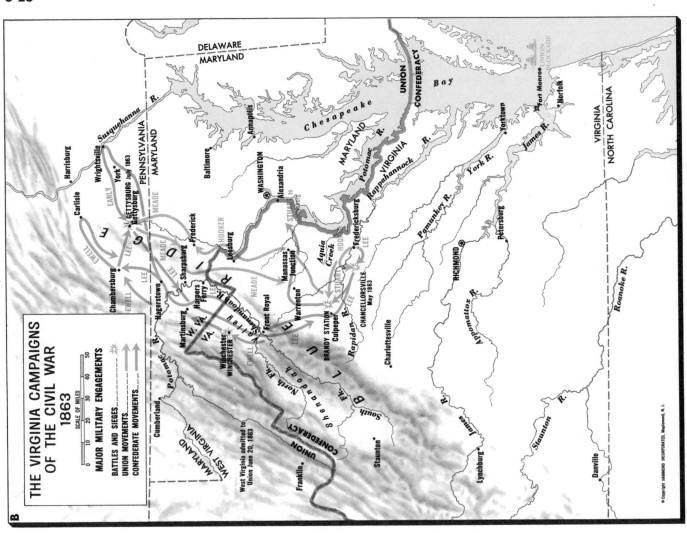

B

THE VIRGINIA CAMPAIGNS OF THE CIVIL WAR 1863

SCALE OF MILES

0 10 20 30 40 50

MAJOR MILITARY ENGAGEMENTS

BATTLES AND SIEGES
UNION MOVEMENTS
CONFEDERATE MOVEMENTS

West Virginia admitted to Union June 20, 1863

© Copyright HAMMOND INCORPORATED, Maplewood, N.J.

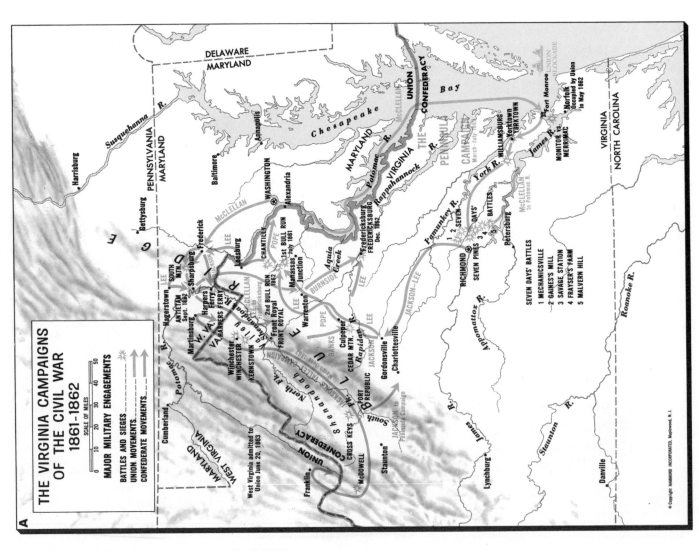

A

THE VIRGINIA CAMPAIGNS OF THE CIVIL WAR 1861-1862

SCALE OF MILES

0 10 20 30 40 50

MAJOR MILITARY ENGAGEMENTS

BATTLES AND SIEGES
UNION MOVEMENTS
CONFEDERATE MOVEMENTS

West Virginia admitted to Union June 20, 1863

SEVEN DAYS' BATTLES

1 MECHANICSVILLE
2 GAINES'S MILL
3 SAVAGE STATION
4 FRAYSER'S FARM
5 MALVERN HILL

© Copyright HAMMOND INCORPORATED, Maplewood, N.J.

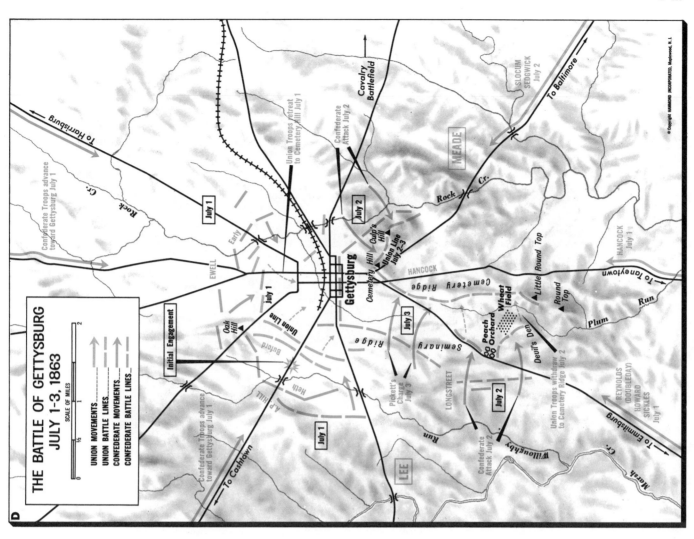

THE BATTLE OF GETTYSBURG JULY 1-3, 1863

SCALE OF MILES

UNION MOVEMENTS
UNION BATTLE LINES
CONFEDERATE MOVEMENTS
CONFEDERATE BATTLE LINES

Initial Engagement

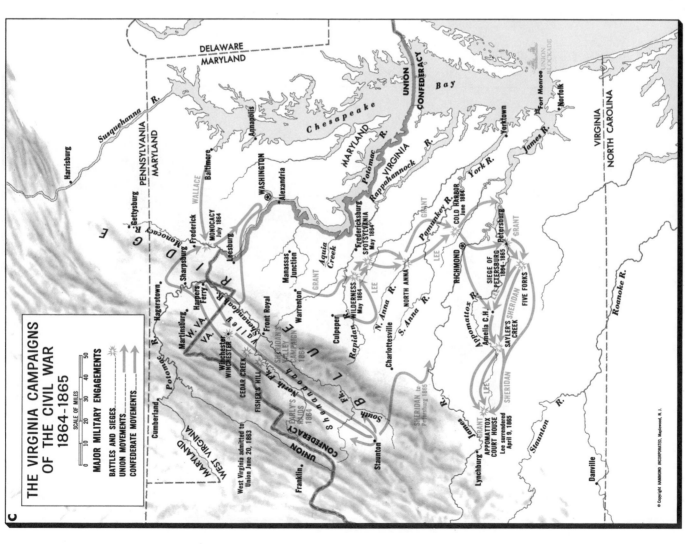

THE VIRGINIA CAMPAIGNS OF THE CIVIL WAR 1864-1865

SCALE OF MILES
0   10   20   30   40   50

MAJOR MILITARY ENGAGEMENTS

BATTLES AND SIEGES
UNION MOVEMENTS
CONFEDERATE MOVEMENTS

West Virginia admitted to Union June 20, 1863

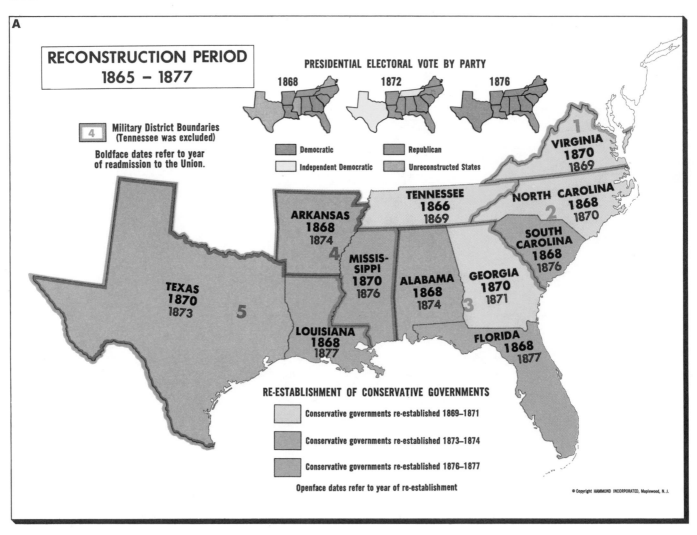

RECONSTRUCTION PERIOD 1865 – 1877

PRESIDENTIAL ELECTORAL VOTE BY PARTY

1868   1872   1876

4 Military District Boundaries
(Tennessee was excluded)

Boldface dates refer to year
of readmission to the Union.

Democratic   Republican
Independent Democratic   Unreconstructed States

VIRGINIA **1870** 1869

TENNESSEE **1866** 1869

NORTH CAROLINA **1868** 1870

ARKANSAS **1868** 1874

SOUTH CAROLINA **1868** 1876

MISSIS-SIPPI **1870** 1876

ALABAMA **1868** 1874

GEORGIA **1870** 1871

TEXAS **1870** 1873

LOUISIANA **1868** 1877

FLORIDA **1868** 1877

RE-ESTABLISHMENT OF CONSERVATIVE GOVERNMENTS

Conservative governments re-established 1869–1871

Conservative governments re-established 1873–1874

Conservative governments re-established 1876–1877

Openface dates refer to year of re-establishment

© Copyright HAMMOND INCORPORATED, Maplewood, N.J.

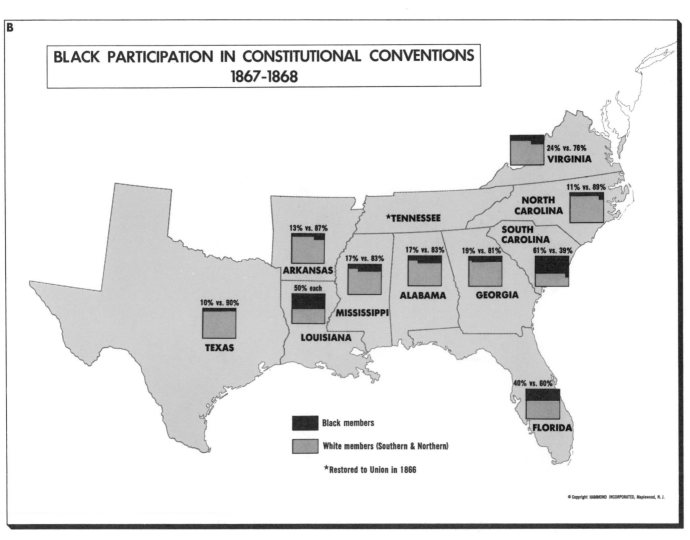

BLACK PARTICIPATION IN CONSTITUTIONAL CONVENTIONS 1867-1868

24% vs. 76% VIRGINIA

11% vs. 89% NORTH CAROLINA

★TENNESSEE

SOUTH CAROLINA

13% vs. 87% ARKANSAS

17% vs. 83% ALABAMA

19% vs. 81% GEORGIA

61% vs. 39%

50% each MISSISSIPPI

10% vs. 90% TEXAS

LOUISIANA

40% vs. 60% FLORIDA

Black members

White members (Southern & Northern)

*Restored to Union in 1866

© Copyright HAMMOND INCORPORATED, Maplewood, N.J.

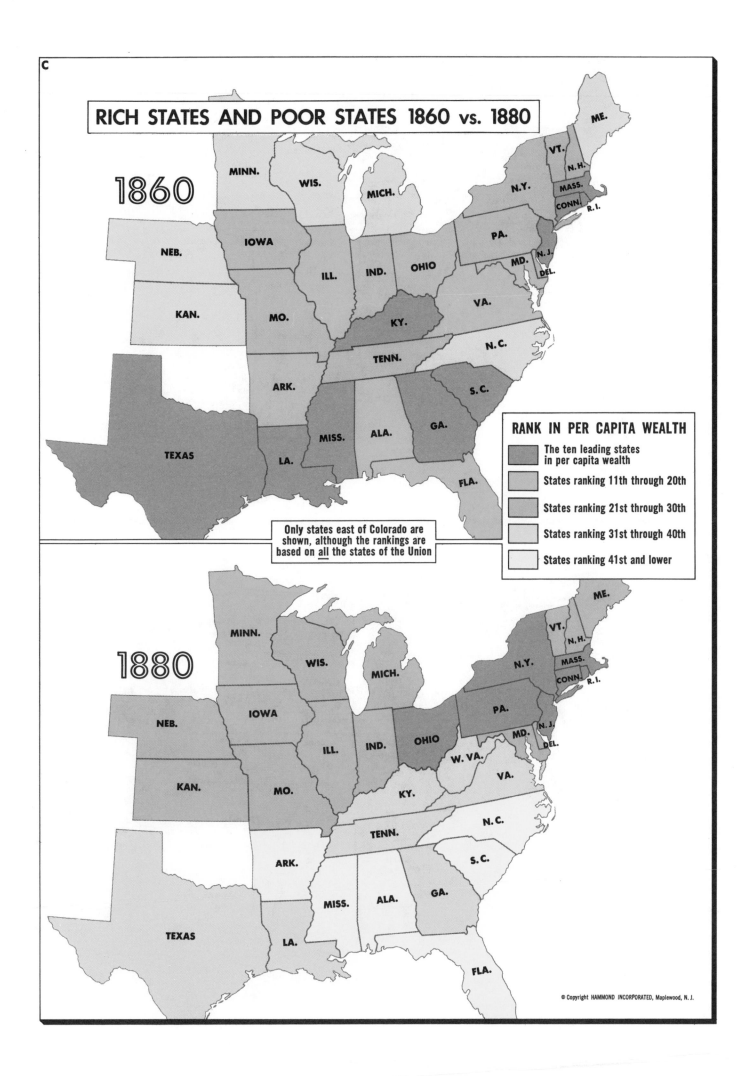

RICH STATES AND POOR STATES 1860 vs. 1880

1860

MINN.
WIS.
MICH.
ME.
VT.
N.H.
N.Y.
MASS.
CONN.
R.I.
NEB.
IOWA
PA.
N.J.
DEL.
MD.
ILL.
IND.
OHIO
KAN.
MO.
KY.
VA.
N.C.
TENN.
ARK.
S.C.
TEXAS
MISS.
ALA.
GA.
LA.
FLA.

RANK IN PER CAPITA WEALTH

- The ten leading states in per capita wealth
- States ranking 11th through 20th
- States ranking 21st through 30th
- States ranking 31st through 40th
- States ranking 41st and lower

Only states east of Colorado are shown, although the rankings are based on all the states of the Union

1880

MINN.
WIS.
MICH.
ME.
VT.
N.H.
N.Y.
MASS.
CONN.
R.I.
NEB.
IOWA
PA.
N.J.
DEL.
MD.
ILL.
IND.
OHIO
W. VA.
KAN.
MO.
KY.
VA.
N.C.
TENN.
ARK.
S.C.
GA.
TEXAS
MISS.
ALA.
LA.
FLA.

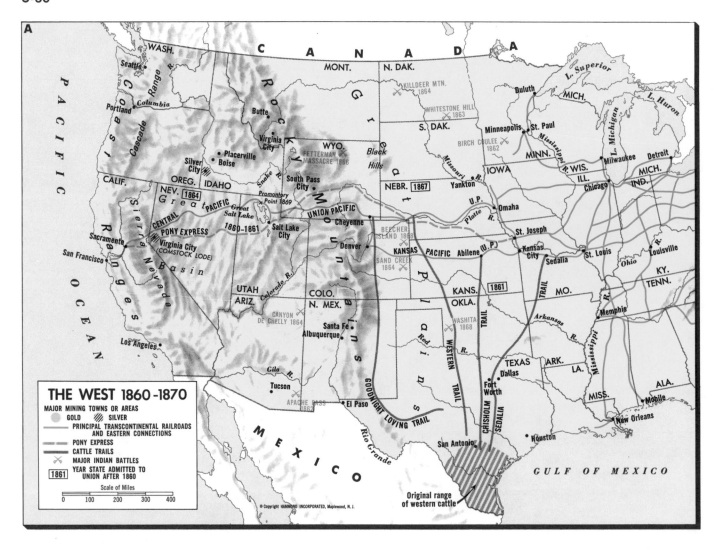

A

THE WEST 1860-1870

MAJOR MINING TOWNS OR AREAS
- GOLD
- SILVER
- PRINCIPAL TRANSCONTINENTAL RAILROADS AND EASTERN CONNECTIONS
- PONY EXPRESS
- CATTLE TRAILS
- ✕ MAJOR INDIAN BATTLES
- 1861 YEAR STATE ADMITTED TO UNION AFTER 1860

Scale of Miles
0 100 200 300 400

© Copyright HAMMOND INCORPORATED, Maplewood, N.J.

Original range of western cattle

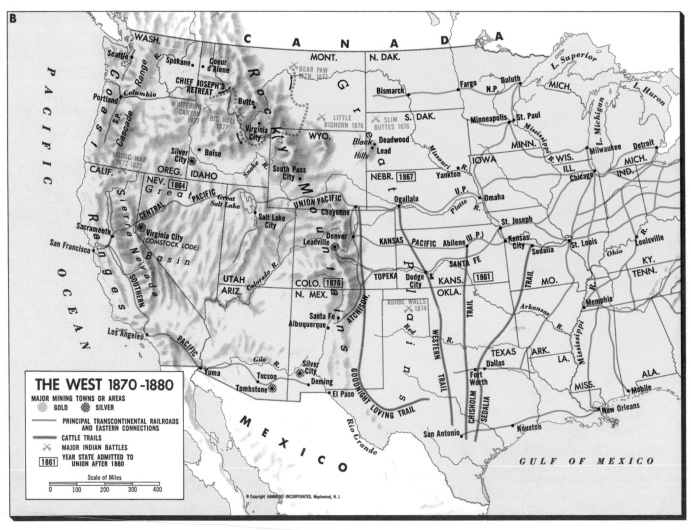

B

THE WEST 1870-1880

MAJOR MINING TOWNS OR AREAS
- GOLD
- SILVER
- PRINCIPAL TRANSCONTINENTAL RAILROADS AND EASTERN CONNECTIONS
- CATTLE TRAILS
- ✕ MAJOR INDIAN BATTLES
- 1861 YEAR STATE ADMITTED TO UNION AFTER 1860

Scale of Miles
0 100 200 300 400

© Copyright HAMMOND INCORPORATED, Maplewood, N.J.

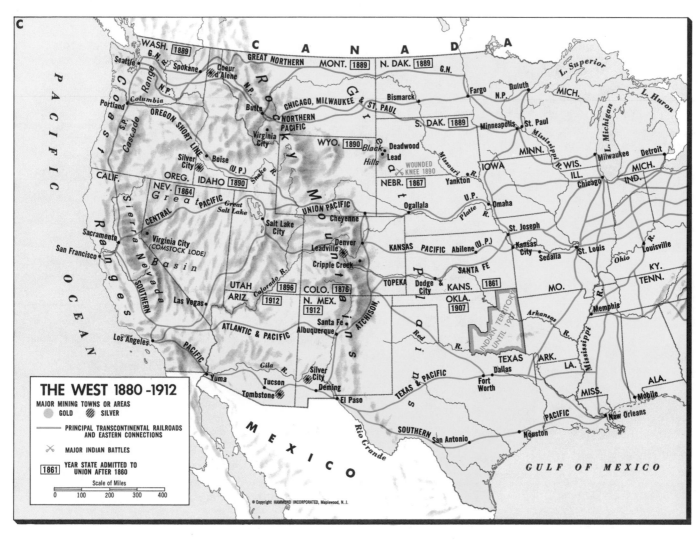

THE WEST 1880-1912

MAJOR MINING TOWNS OR AREAS
- GOLD
- SILVER

— PRINCIPAL TRANSCONTINENTAL RAILROADS AND EASTERN CONNECTIONS

✕ MAJOR INDIAN BATTLES

1861 YEAR STATE ADMITTED TO UNION AFTER 1860

Scale of Miles
0   100   200   300   400

© Copyright HAMMOND INCORPORATED, Maplewood, N.J.

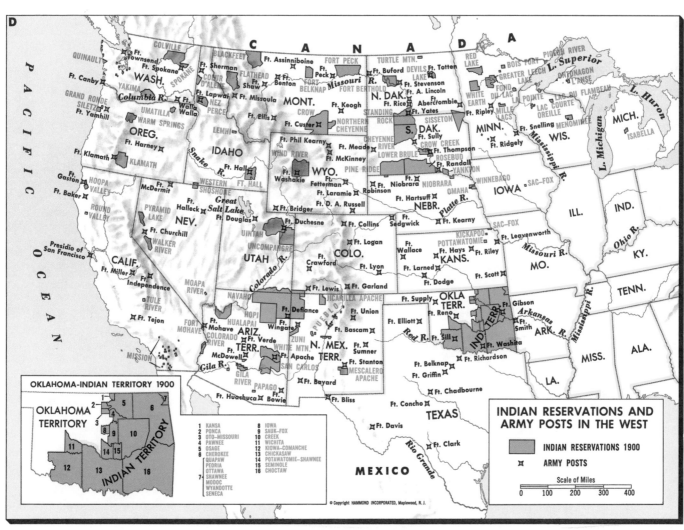

INDIAN RESERVATIONS AND ARMY POSTS IN THE WEST

■ INDIAN RESERVATIONS 1900

✕ ARMY POSTS

Scale of Miles
0   100   200   300   400

OKLAHOMA-INDIAN TERRITORY 1900

OKLAHOMA TERRITORY

INDIAN TERRITORY

1 KANSA
2 PONCA
3 OTO-MISSOURI
4 PAWNEE
5 OSAGE
6 CHEROKEE
7 QUAPAW
  PEORIA
  OTTAWA
  SHAWNEE
  MODOC
  WYANDOTTE
  SENECA
8 IOWA
9 SAUK-FOX
10 CREEK
11 WICHITA
12 KIOWA-COMANCHE
13 CHICKASAW
14 POTAWATOMIE-SHAWNEE
15 SEMINOLE
16 CHOCTAW

© Copyright HAMMOND INCORPORATED, Maplewood, N.J.

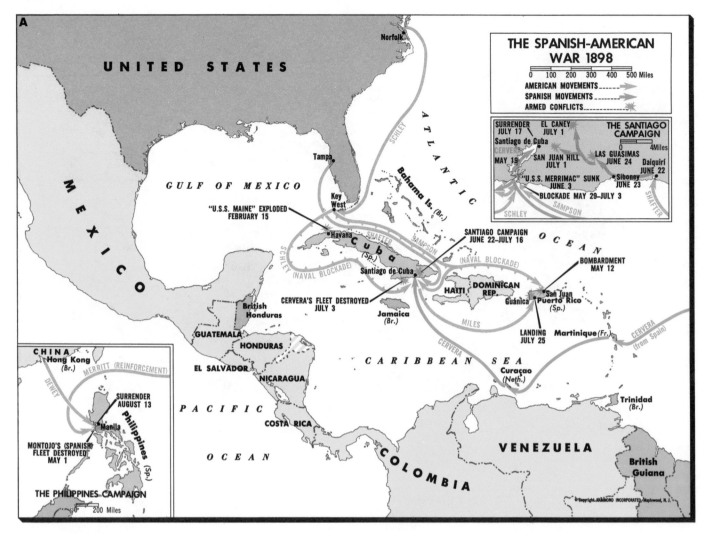

A

UNITED STATES

THE SPANISH-AMERICAN
WAR 1898

0   100   200   300   400   500 Miles

AMERICAN MOVEMENTS
SPANISH MOVEMENTS
ARMED CONFLICTS

THE SANTIAGO
CAMPAIGN

SURRENDER   EL CANEY
JULY 17   JULY 1
Santiago de Cuba
CERVERA   SAN JUAN HILL   LAS GUASIMAS
MAY 19   JULY 1   JUNE 24   Daiquiri
                                            JUNE 22
"U.S.S. MERRIMAC" SUNK   Siboney
JUNE 23   JUNE 23
BLOCKADE MAY 29-JULY 3
SCHLEY   SAMPSON   SHAFTER

Norfolk

MEXICO

GULF OF MEXICO

Tampa

Key
West

"U.S.S. MAINE" EXPLODED
FEBRUARY 15

Havana Cuba
        (Sp.)
SHAFTER
Santiago de Cuba
SCHLEY (NAVAL BLOCKADE)

Bahama Is.
(Br.)

SAMPSON

SANTIAGO CAMPAIGN
JUNE 22-JULY 16

(NAVAL BLOCKADE)

BOMBARDMENT
MAY 12

ATLANTIC

OCEAN

CERVERA'S FLEET DESTROYED
JULY 3

HAITI   DOMINICAN
        REP.   Guánica San Juan
        Jamaica   Puerto Rico
        (Br.)   (Sp.)
        MILES
                    LANDING   Martinique (Fr.)   CERVERA
                    JULY 25   (from Spain)

British
Honduras

GUATEMALA

HONDURAS

EL SALVADOR

NICARAGUA

CARIBBEAN   SEA

Curaçao
(Neth.)

Trinidad
(Br.)

CHINA
Hong Kong
(Br.)

MERRITT (REINFORCEMENT)

DEWEY

SURRENDER
AUGUST 13

Manila

MONTOJO'S (SPANISH)
FLEET DESTROYED
MAY 1

Philippines
(Sp.)

THE PHILIPPINES CAMPAIGN

0   200 Miles

PACIFIC

OCEAN

COSTA RICA

VENEZUELA

COLOMBIA

British
Guiana

© Copyright HAMMOND INCORPORATED, Maplewood, N.J.

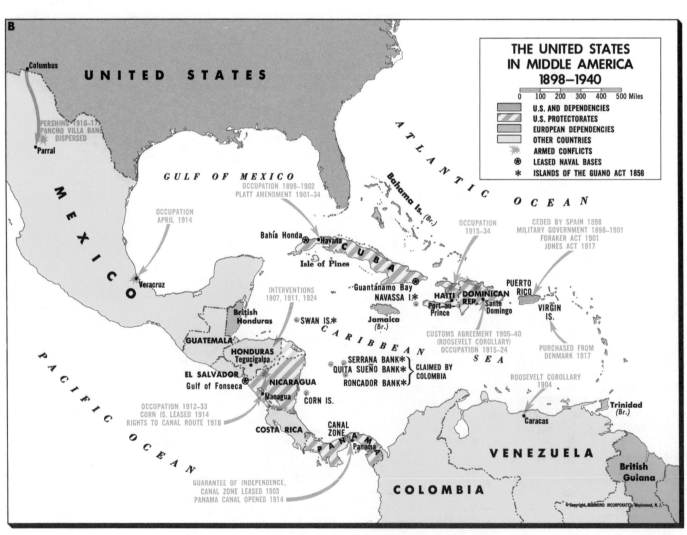

B

Columbus

UNITED STATES

PERSHING 1916-17
PANCHO VILLA BAND
DISPERSED

Parral

MEXICO

GULF OF MEXICO

OCCUPATION 1898-1902
PLATT AMENDMENT 1901-34

OCCUPATION
APRIL 1914

Veracruz

THE UNITED STATES
IN MIDDLE AMERICA
1898-1940

0   100   200   300   400   500 Miles

U.S. AND DEPENDENCIES
U.S. PROTECTORATES
EUROPEAN DEPENDENCIES
OTHER COUNTRIES
ARMED CONFLICTS
LEASED NAVAL BASES
ISLANDS OF THE GUANO ACT 1856

Bahama Is.
(Br.)

ATLANTIC

OCEAN

OCCUPATION
1915-34

CEDED BY SPAIN 1898
MILITARY GOVERNMENT 1898-1901
FORAKER ACT 1901
JONES ACT 1917

Bahía Honda   Havana
CUBA
Isle of Pines

INTERVENTIONS
1907, 1911, 1924

British
Honduras

GUATEMALA

HONDURAS
Tegucigalpa

EL SALVADOR
Gulf of Fonseca

OCCUPATION 1912-33
CORN IS. LEASED 1914
RIGHTS TO CANAL ROUTE 1916

Guantánamo Bay
NAVASSA I.

SWAN IS.

Jamaica
(Br.)

NICARAGUA
Managua

CORN IS.

COSTA RICA

SERRANA BANK
QUITA SUEÑO BANK   CLAIMED BY
RONCADOR BANK   COLOMBIA

HAITI   DOMINICAN
Port-au-   REP.
Prince   Santo
                Domingo

PUERTO
RICO

VIRGIN
IS.

CUSTOMS AGREEMENT 1905-40
(ROOSEVELT COROLLARY)
OCCUPATION 1915-24

PURCHASED FROM
DENMARK 1917

ROOSEVELT COROLLARY
1904

CARIBBEAN   SEA

CANAL
ZONE
Panama

PANAMA

GUARANTEE OF INDEPENDENCE,
CANAL ZONE LEASED 1903
PANAMA CANAL OPENED 1914

PACIFIC

OCEAN

Trinidad
(Br.)

Caracas

VENEZUELA

COLOMBIA

British
Guiana

© Copyright HAMMOND INCORPORATED, Maplewood, N.J.

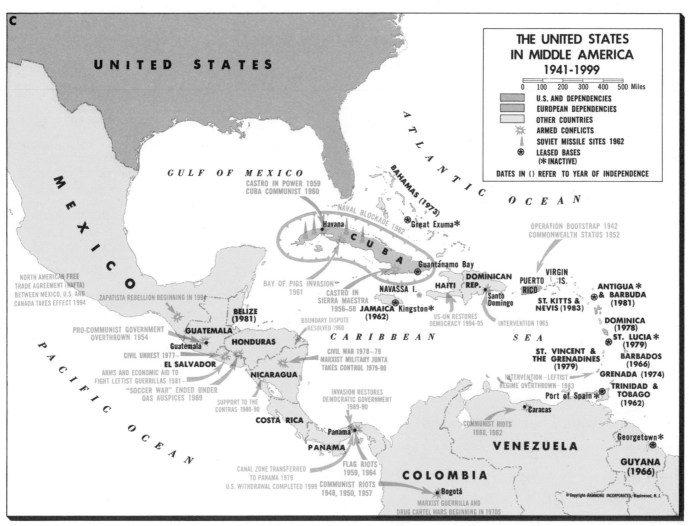

C

UNITED STATES

GULF OF MEXICO

M E X I C O

PACIFIC OCEAN

NORTH AMERICAN FREE
TRADE AGREEMENT (NAFTA)
BETWEEN MEXICO, U.S. AND
CANADA TAKES EFFECT 1994

ZAPATISTA REBELLION BEGINNING IN 1994

PRO-COMMUNIST GOVERNMENT
OVERTHROWN 1954

GUATEMALA

Guatemala

CIVIL UNREST 1977

EL SALVADOR

ARMS AND ECONOMIC AID TO
FIGHT LEFTIST GUERRILLAS 1981

"SOCCER WAR" ENDED UNDER
OAS AUSPICES 1969

SUPPORT TO THE
CONTRAS 1980-90

COSTA RICA

PANAMA

CANAL ZONE TRANSFERRED
TO PANAMA 1979

U.S. WITHDRAWAL COMPLETED 1999

BELIZE
(1981)

HONDURAS

NICARAGUA

BOUNDARY DISPUTE
RESOLVED 1960

CIVIL WAR 1978-79
MARXIST MILITARY JUNTA
TAKES CONTROL 1979-90

INVASION RESTORES
DEMOCRATIC GOVERNMENT
1989-90

Panama

FLAG RIOTS
1959, 1964

COMMUNIST RIOTS
1948, 1950, 1957

CASTRO IN POWER 1959
CUBA COMMUNIST 1960

BAHAMAS (1973)

NAVAL BLOCKADE 1962

Havana

Great Exuma*

CUBA

Guantánamo Bay

BAY OF PIGS INVASION
1961

CASTRO IN
SIERRA MAESTRA
1956-58

NAVASSA I.

HAITI

JAMAICA Kingston*
(1962)

US-UN RESTORES
DEMOCRACY 1994-95

**DOMINICAN
REP.**

Santo
Domingo

INTERVENTION 1965

ATLANTIC OCEAN

OPERATION BOOTSTRAP 1942
COMMONWEALTH STATUS 1952

**PUERTO
RICO**

**VIRGIN
IS.**

ANTIGUA *
**& BARBUDA
(1981)**

**ST. KITTS &
NEVIS (1983)**

**DOMINICA
(1978)**

ST. LUCIA *
(1979)

**ST. VINCENT &
THE GRENADINES
(1979)**

**BARBADOS
(1966)**

GRENADA (1974)

**TRINIDAD &
TOBAGO
(1962)**

INTERVENTION—LEFTIST
REGIME OVERTHROWN—1983

Port of Spain *

C A R I B B E A N   S E A

COMMUNIST RIOTS
1960, 1962

Caracas

VENEZUELA

Georgetown*

**GUYANA
(1966)**

COLOMBIA

Bogotá

MARXIST GUERRILLA AND
DRUG CARTEL WARS BEGINNING IN 1970S

© Copyright HAMMOND INCORPORATED, Maplewood, N.J.

THE UNITED STATES
IN MIDDLE AMERICA
1941-1999

0   100   200   300   400   500 Miles

U.S. AND DEPENDENCIES
EUROPEAN DEPENDENCIES
OTHER COUNTRIES
ARMED CONFLICTS
SOVIET MISSILE SITES 1962
LEASED BASES
(* INACTIVE)

DATES IN ( ) REFER TO YEAR OF INDEPENDENCE

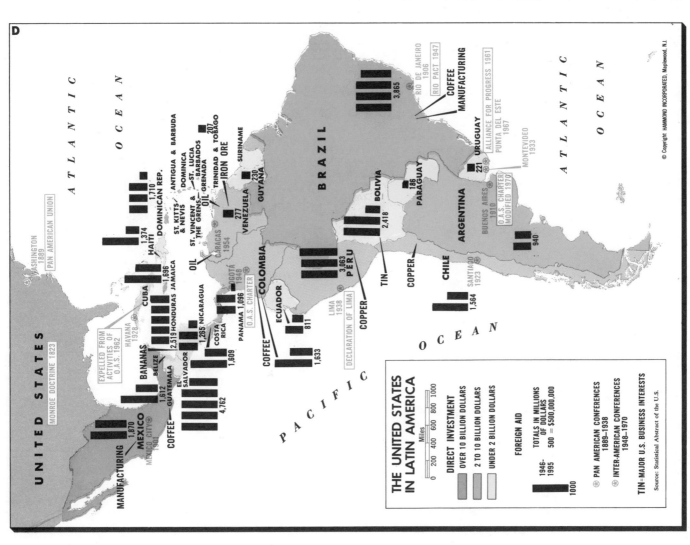

D

UNITED STATES

MONROE DOCTRINE 1823

MEXICO

MANUFACTURING

1,870

MEXICO CITY

1901

COFFEE

**ATLANTIC
OCEAN**

WASHINGTON
1889
PAN AMERICAN UNION

EXPELLED FROM
ACTIVITIES OF
O.A.S. 1962

HAVANA
1928

DOMINICAN REP.

1,710

1,374

HAITI

CUBA

1,696

JAMAICA

BANANAS

BELIZE

1,612

GUATEMALA

EL SALVADOR

4,762

2,519 HONDURAS

1,285 NICARAGUA

1,609

1,096 COSTA RICA

Panama 1,096

O.A.S. CHARTER

ANTIGUA & BARBUDA

DOMINICA

ST. LUCIA

BARBADOS

GRENADA

TRINIDAD & TOBAGO

IRON ORE

207

SURINAME

230

GUYANA

277

VENEZUELA

OIL

**ST. KITTS
& NEVIS**

**ST. VINCENT &
THE GRENS.**

CARACAS
1954

OIL

BOGOTÁ 1948

COLOMBIA

COFFEE

ECUADOR

811

1,633

COFFEE

LIMA
1938

DECLARATION OF LIMA

3,063

PERU

TIN

COPPER

BRAZIL

3,865

RIO DE JANEIRO
1906

RIO PACT 1947

**COFFEE
MANUFACTURING**

ALLIANCE FOR PROGRESS 1961

PUNTA DEL ESTE
1967

MONTEVIDEO
1933

URUGUAY

221

186

PARAGUAY

BOLIVIA

2,418

COPPER

BUENOS AIRES
1910

O.A.S. CHARTER
MODIFIED 1970

ARGENTINA

940

CHILE

1,564

COPPER

SANTIAGO
1923

**ATLANTIC

OCEAN**

**PACIFIC
OCEAN**

© Copyright HAMMOND INCORPORATED, Maplewood, N.J.

THE UNITED STATES
IN LATIN AMERICA

Miles
0   200   400   600   800   1000

DIRECT INVESTMENT
OVER 10 BILLION DOLLARS
2 TO 10 BILLION DOLLARS
UNDER 2 BILLION DOLLARS

FOREIGN AID
TOTALS IN MILLIONS
OF DOLLARS
500 = $500,000,000

1946-
1995

1000

⊛ PAN AMERICAN CONFERENCES
1889-1938
⊛ INTER-AMERICAN CONFERENCES
1948-1970

TIN = MAJOR U.S. BUSINESS INTERESTS

Source: Statistical Abstract of the U.S.

A

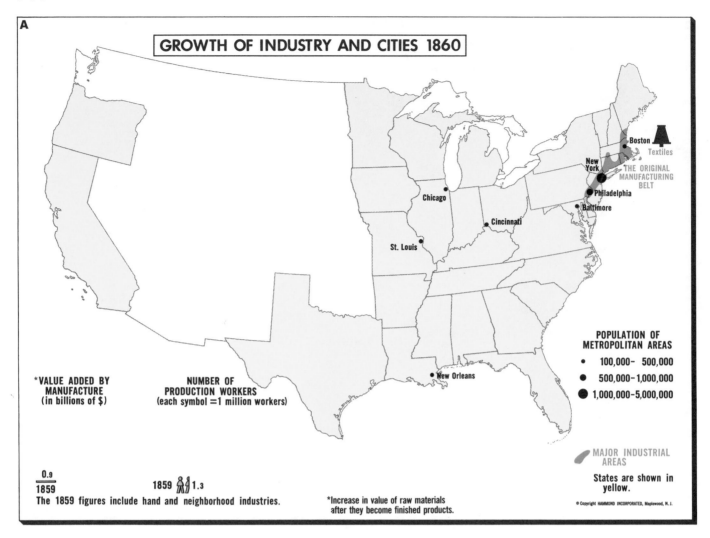

GROWTH OF INDUSTRY AND CITIES 1860

Boston
Textiles

New
York
THE ORIGINAL
MANUFACTURING
BELT

Chicago

Philadelphia
Baltimore

Cincinnati

St. Louis

New Orleans

**POPULATION OF
METROPOLITAN AREAS**

· 100,000 – 500,000

● 500,000 – 1,000,000

● 1,000,000 – 5,000,000

***VALUE ADDED BY
MANUFACTURE**
(in billions of $)

**NUMBER OF
PRODUCTION WORKERS**
(each symbol =1 million workers)

MAJOR INDUSTRIAL
AREAS

States are shown in
yellow.

$\frac{0.9}{1859}$

1859 ⚥ 1.3

The 1859 figures include hand and neighborhood industries.

*Increase in value of raw materials
after they become finished products.

© Copyright HAMMOND INCORPORATED, Maplewood, N. J.

B

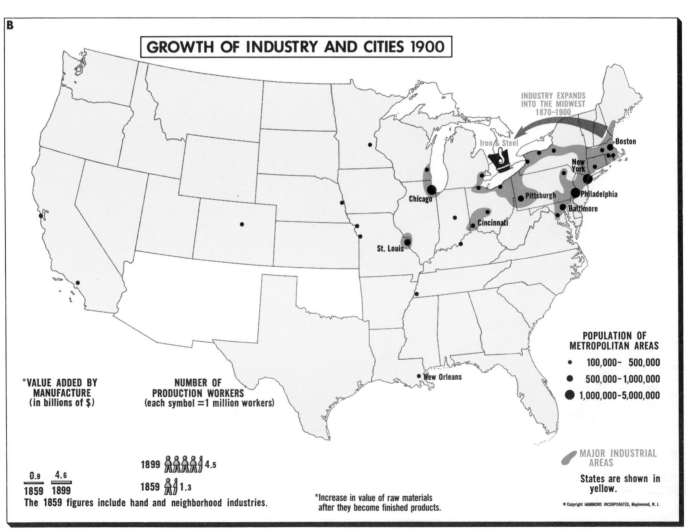

GROWTH OF INDUSTRY AND CITIES 1900

INDUSTRY EXPANDS
INTO THE MIDWEST
1870–1900

Boston

Iron & Steel

New
York

Chicago

Pittsburgh

Philadelphia
Baltimore

Cincinnati

St. Louis

New Orleans

**POPULATION OF
METROPOLITAN AREAS**

· 100,000 – 500,000

● 500,000 – 1,000,000

● 1,000,000 – 5,000,000

***VALUE ADDED BY
MANUFACTURE**
(in billions of $)

**NUMBER OF
PRODUCTION WORKERS**
(each symbol =1 million workers)

1899 👥👥👥👥 4.5

1859 👤 1.3

$\frac{0.9}{1859}$ $\frac{4.6}{1899}$

The 1859 figures include hand and neighborhood industries.

*Increase in value of raw materials
after they become finished products.

MAJOR INDUSTRIAL
AREAS

States are shown in
yellow.

© Copyright HAMMOND INCORPORATED, Maplewood, N. J.

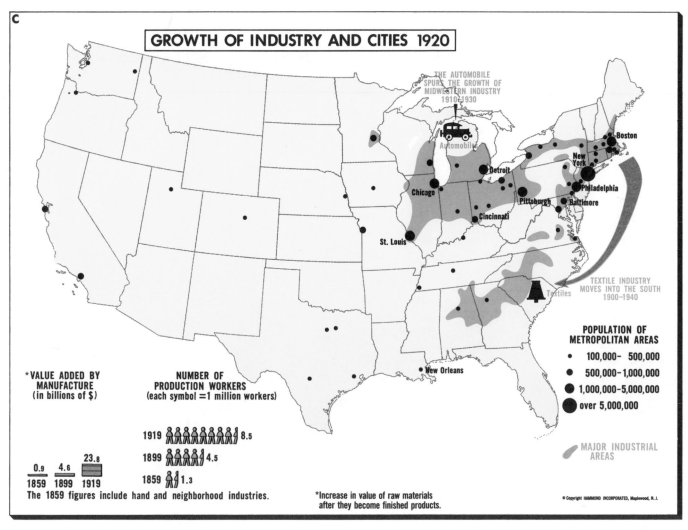

C

GROWTH OF INDUSTRY AND CITIES 1920

THE AUTOMOBILE SPURS THE GROWTH OF MIDWESTERN INDUSTRY 1910–1930

Automobiles

Boston
New York
Detroit
Philadelphia
Chicago
Pittsburgh
Baltimore
Cincinnati
St. Louis

TEXTILE INDUSTRY MOVES INTO THE SOUTH 1900–1940

Textiles

New Orleans

POPULATION OF METROPOLITAN AREAS

- 100,000– 500,000
- 500,000–1,000,000
- 1,000,000–5,000,000
- over 5,000,000

MAJOR INDUSTRIAL AREAS

*VALUE ADDED BY MANUFACTURE (in billions of $)

NUMBER OF PRODUCTION WORKERS (each symbol =1 million workers)

1919   8.5
1899   4.5
1859   1.3

0.9   4.6   23.8
1859 1899 1919

The 1859 figures include hand and neighborhood industries.

*Increase in value of raw materials after they become finished products.

© Copyright HAMMOND INCORPORATED, Maplewood, N.J.

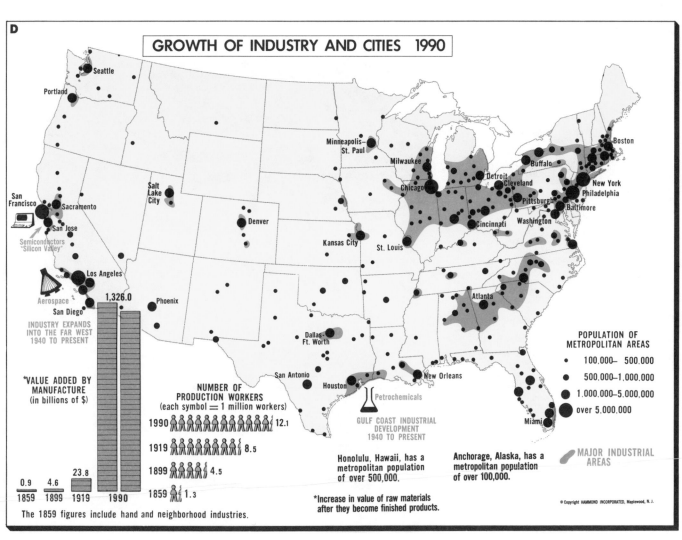

D

GROWTH OF INDUSTRY AND CITIES   1990

Seattle
Portland

Minneapolis–St. Paul
Milwaukee
Buffalo
Boston
Detroit
Cleveland
New York
Chicago
Pittsburgh
Philadelphia
Baltimore
Cincinnati   Washington

San Francisco
Sacramento
San Jose
Semiconductors "Silicon Valley"

Salt Lake City

Denver

Kansas City
St. Louis

Los Angeles

Aerospace

1,326.0

San Diego
Phoenix

INDUSTRY EXPANDS INTO THE FAR WEST 1940 TO PRESENT

Atlanta

San Antonio
Dallas–Ft. Worth

Houston   Petrochemicals
New Orleans

GULF COAST INDUSTRIAL DEVELOPMENT 1940 TO PRESENT

Miami

*VALUE ADDED BY MANUFACTURE (in billions of $)

NUMBER OF PRODUCTION WORKERS (each symbol = 1 million workers)

1990   12.1
1919   8.5
1899   4.5
1859   1.3

0.9   4.6   23.8
1859 1899 1919   1990

The 1859 figures include hand and neighborhood industries.

Honolulu, Hawaii, has a metropolitan population of over 500,000.

Anchorage, Alaska, has a metropolitan population of over 100,000.

*Increase in value of raw materials after they become finished products.

POPULATION OF METROPOLITAN AREAS

- 100,000– 500,000
- 500,000–1,000,000
- 1,000,000–5,000,000
- over 5,000,000

MAJOR INDUSTRIAL AREAS

© Copyright HAMMOND INCORPORATED, Maplewood, N.J.

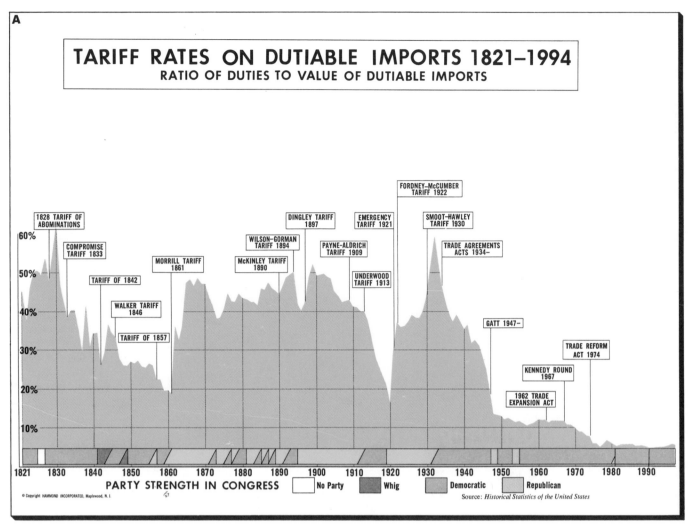

A

TARIFF RATES ON DUTIABLE IMPORTS 1821–1994
RATIO OF DUTIES TO VALUE OF DUTIABLE IMPORTS

FORDNEY–McCUMBER TARIFF 1922

1828 TARIFF OF ABOMINATIONS

DINGLEY TARIFF 1897

EMERGENCY TARIFF 1921

SMOOT–HAWLEY TARIFF 1930

COMPROMISE TARIFF 1833

WILSON–GORMAN TARIFF 1894

PAYNE–ALDRICH TARIFF 1909

TRADE AGREEMENTS ACTS 1934–

MORRILL TARIFF 1861

McKINLEY TARIFF 1890

TARIFF OF 1842

UNDERWOOD TARIFF 1913

WALKER TARIFF 1846

GATT 1947–

TARIFF OF 1857

TRADE REFORM ACT 1974

KENNEDY ROUND 1967

1962 TRADE EXPANSION ACT

60%
50%
40%
30%
20%
10%

1821   1830   1840   1850   1860   1870   1880   1890   1900   1910   1920   1930   1940   1950   1960   1970   1980   1990

PARTY STRENGTH IN CONGRESS — No Party — Whig — Democratic — Republican

© Copyright HAMMOND INCORPORATED, Maplewood, N.J.

Source: *Historical Statistics of the United States*

B

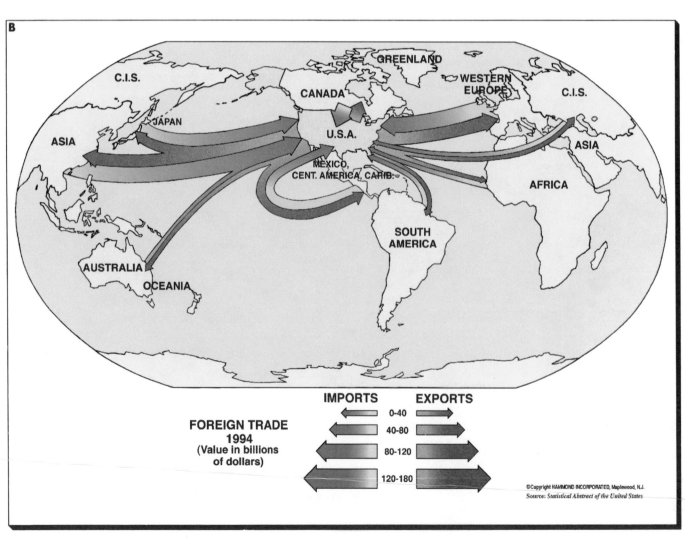

GREENLAND

C.I.S.

WESTERN EUROPE

CANADA

C.I.S.

JAPAN

U.S.A.

ASIA

ASIA

MEXICO, CENT. AMERICA, CARIB.

AFRICA

SOUTH AMERICA

AUSTRALIA

OCEANIA

IMPORTS   EXPORTS

FOREIGN TRADE
1994
(Value in billions
of dollars)

0–40
40–80
80–120
120–180

©Copyright HAMMOND INCORPORATED, Maplewood, N.J.

Source: *Statistical Abstract of the United States*

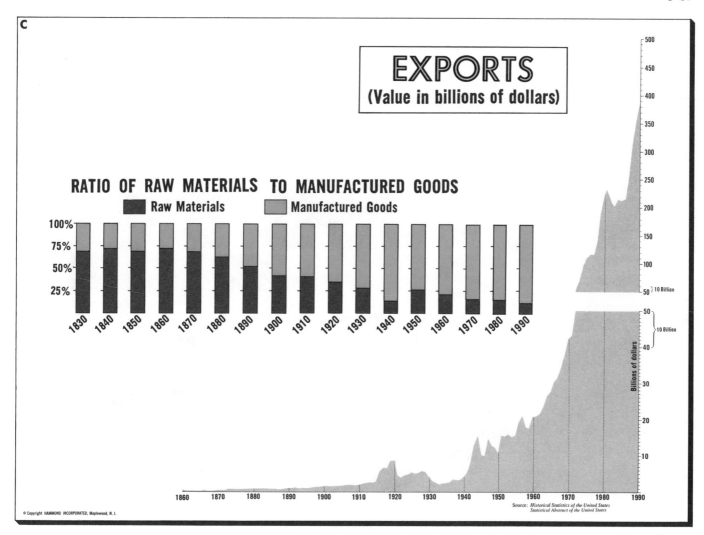

C

EXPORTS
(Value in billions of dollars)

RATIO OF RAW MATERIALS TO MANUFACTURED GOODS
Raw Materials   Manufactured Goods

Source: *Historical Statistics of the United States*
Statistical Abstract of the United States

© Copyright HAMMOND INCORPORATED, Maplewood, N. J.

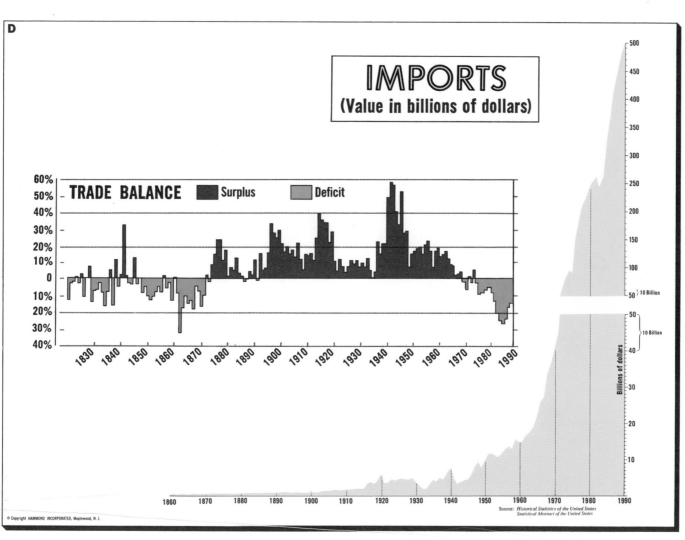

D

IMPORTS
(Value in billions of dollars)

TRADE BALANCE   Surplus   Deficit

Source: *Historical Statistics of the United States*
Statistical Abstract of the United States

© Copyright HAMMOND INCORPORATED, Maplewood, N. J.

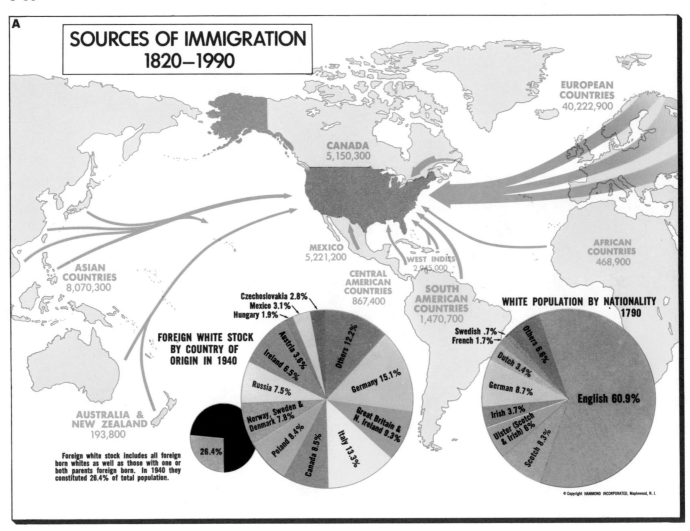

SOURCES OF IMMIGRATION 1820–1990

EUROPEAN COUNTRIES 40,222,900

CANADA 5,150,300

MEXICO 5,221,200

WEST INDIES 2,945,000

CENTRAL AMERICAN COUNTRIES 867,400

SOUTH AMERICAN COUNTRIES 1,470,700

AFRICAN COUNTRIES 468,900

ASIAN COUNTRIES 8,070,300

AUSTRALIA & NEW ZEALAND 193,800

FOREIGN WHITE STOCK BY COUNTRY OF ORIGIN IN 1940

Czechoslovakia 2.8%
Mexico 3.1%
Hungary 1.9%
Austria 3.6%
Ireland 6.5%
Russia 7.5%
Norway, Sweden & Denmark 7.8%
Poland 8.4%
Canada 8.5%
Italy 13.3%
Great Britain & N. Ireland 9.3%
Germany 15.1%
Others 12.2%

26.4%

Foreign white stock includes all foreign born whites as well as those with one or both parents foreign born. In 1940 they constituted 26.4% of total population.

WHITE POPULATION BY NATIONALITY 1790

Swedish .7%
French 1.7%
Others 6.6%
Dutch 3.4%
German 8.7%
Irish 3.7%
Ulster (Scotch & Irish) 6%
Scotch 8.3%
English 60.9%

© Copyright HAMMOND INCORPORATED, Maplewood, N. J.

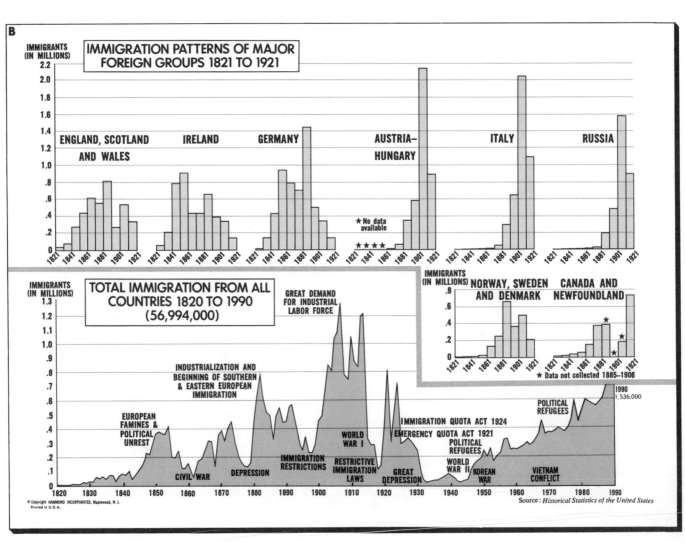

IMMIGRATION PATTERNS OF MAJOR FOREIGN GROUPS 1821 TO 1921

IMMIGRANTS (IN MILLIONS)

ENGLAND, SCOTLAND AND WALES

IRELAND

GERMANY

AUSTRIA–HUNGARY ★ No data available ★★★★

ITALY

RUSSIA

TOTAL IMMIGRATION FROM ALL COUNTRIES 1820 TO 1990 (56,994,000)

IMMIGRANTS (IN MILLIONS)

GREAT DEMAND FOR INDUSTRIAL LABOR FORCE

INDUSTRIALIZATION AND BEGINNING OF SOUTHERN & EASTERN EUROPEAN IMMIGRATION

EUROPEAN FAMINES & POLITICAL UNREST

CIVIL WAR

DEPRESSION

IMMIGRATION RESTRICTIONS

RESTRICTIVE IMMIGRATION LAWS

WORLD WAR I

EMERGENCY QUOTA ACT 1921
POLITICAL REFUGEES

IMMIGRATION QUOTA ACT 1924

GREAT DEPRESSION

WORLD WAR II

KOREAN WAR

VIETNAM CONFLICT

POLITICAL REFUGEES

1990 1,536,000

IMMIGRANTS (IN MILLIONS)
NORWAY, SWEDEN AND DENMARK
CANADA AND NEWFOUNDLAND
★ Data not collected 1885–1906

© Copyright HAMMOND INCORPORATED, Maplewood, N. J.
Printed in U.S.A.

Source: Historical Statistics of the United States

DISTRIBUTION OF FOREIGN BORN IN UNITED STATES
1910

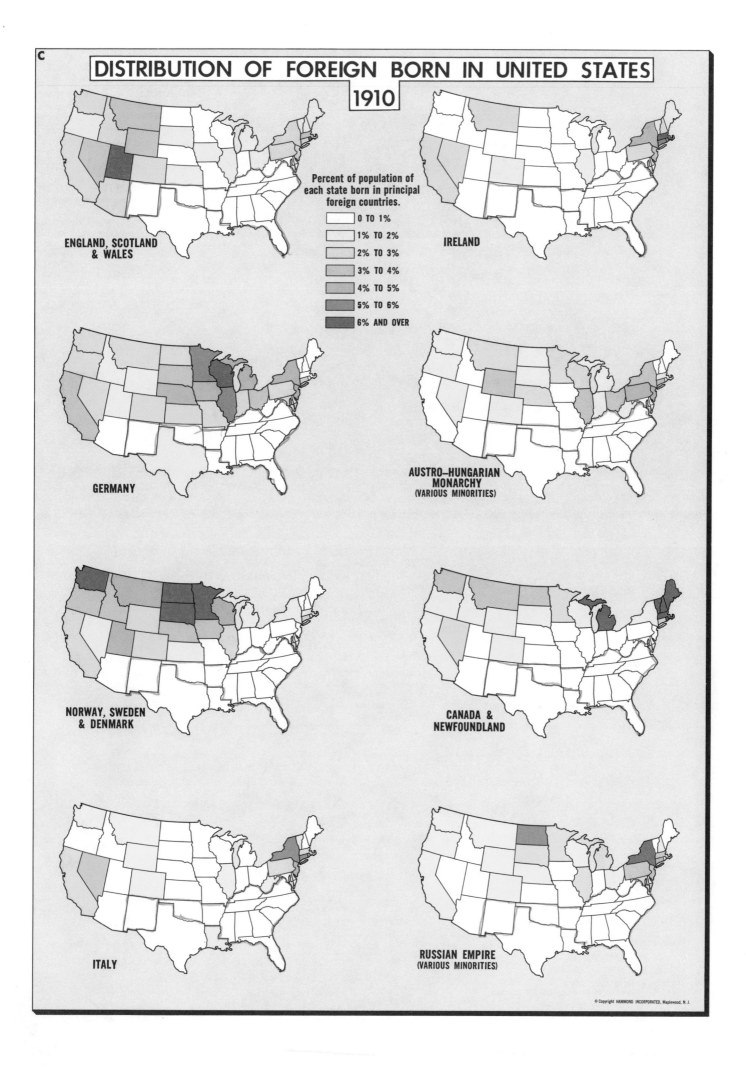

Percent of population of each state born in principal foreign countries.

- 0 TO 1%
- 1% TO 2%
- 2% TO 3%
- 3% TO 4%
- 4% TO 5%
- 5% TO 6%
- 6% AND OVER

ENGLAND, SCOTLAND & WALES

IRELAND

GERMANY

AUSTRO–HUNGARIAN MONARCHY
(VARIOUS MINORITIES)

NORWAY, SWEDEN & DENMARK

CANADA & NEWFOUNDLAND

ITALY

RUSSIAN EMPIRE
(VARIOUS MINORITIES)

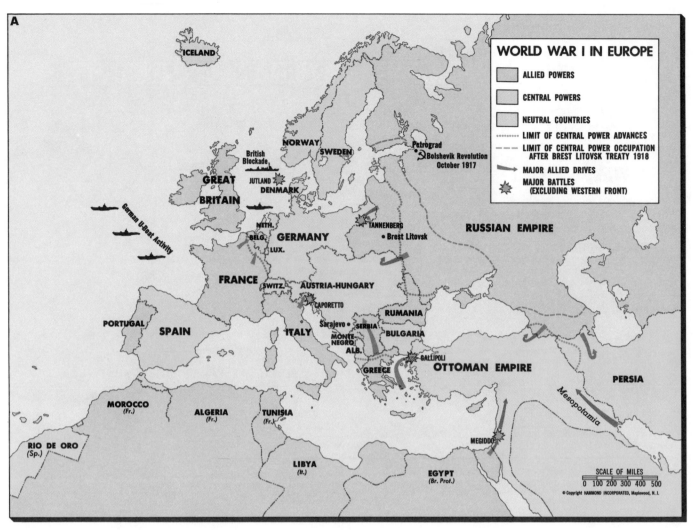

A

ICELAND

NORWAY

SWEDEN

Petrograd
Bolshevik Revolution
October 1917

British
Blockade

**GREAT
BRITAIN**

JUTLAND
DENMARK

German U-Boat Activity

NETH.

BELG.

LUX.

GERMANY

TANNENBERG

• Brest Litovsk

RUSSIAN EMPIRE

FRANCE

SWITZ.

AUSTRIA-HUNGARY

CAPORETTO

PORTUGAL

SPAIN

ITALY

Sarajevo •

MONTE-
NEGRO
ALB.

SERBIA

RUMANIA

BULGARIA

GREECE

GALLIPOLI

OTTOMAN EMPIRE

PERSIA

Mesopotamia

MOROCCO
(Fr.)

ALGERIA
(Fr.)

TUNISIA
(Fr.)

MEGIDDO

RIO DE ORO
(Sp.)

LIBYA
(It.)

EGYPT
(Br. Prot.)

WORLD WAR I IN EUROPE

ALLIED POWERS

CENTRAL POWERS

NEUTRAL COUNTRIES

LIMIT OF CENTRAL POWER ADVANCES

LIMIT OF CENTRAL POWER OCCUPATION
AFTER BREST LITOVSK TREATY 1918

MAJOR ALLIED DRIVES

MAJOR BATTLES
(EXCLUDING WESTERN FRONT)

SCALE OF MILES
0 100 200 300 400 500

© Copyright HAMMOND INCORPORATED, Maplewood, N.J.

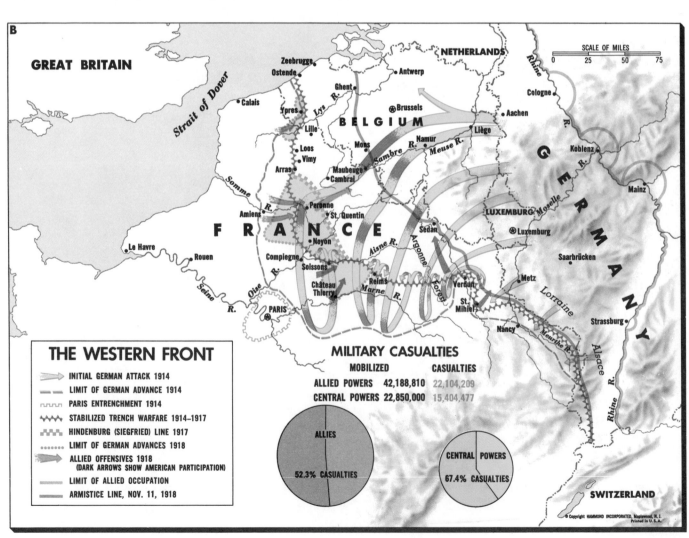

B

GREAT BRITAIN

NETHERLANDS

Rhine R.

SCALE OF MILES
0   25   50   75

Zeebrugge •

Ostende •

• Antwerp

Strait of Dover

• Calais

Ghent •

Brussels

• Aachen

Cologne

Ypres •

BELGIUM

Liège •

• Lille

Namur

Koblenz

Loos •

Mons •

Sambre R.

Meuse R.

G

• Vimy

Maubeuge •

Arras •

Cambrai •

E

Somme

Peronne •

St. Quentin •

Sedan •

LUXEMBURG

Moselle R.

R

Amiens •

F R A N C E

Luxemburg

Mainz

• Le Havre

Rouen

R.

Noyon •

Aisne R.

Argonne
Forest

Metz •

Saarbrücken •

M

Compiegne •

Verdun •

Seine R.

Oise R.

Soissons •

Château
Thierry •

Reims •

Marne R.

St.
Mihiel •

Lorraine

A

Strassburg •

PARIS

Nancy •

Meurthe R.

Rhine R.

Alsace

N

Y

SWITZERLAND

THE WESTERN FRONT

INITIAL GERMAN ATTACK 1914

LIMIT OF GERMAN ADVANCE 1914

PARIS ENTRENCHMENT 1914

STABILIZED TRENCH WARFARE 1914–1917

HINDENBURG (SIEGFRIED) LINE 1917

LIMIT OF GERMAN ADVANCES 1918

ALLIED OFFENSIVES 1918
(DARK ARROWS SHOW AMERICAN PARTICIPATION)

LIMIT OF ALLIED OCCUPATION

ARMISTICE LINE, NOV. 11, 1918

MILITARY CASUALTIES

	MOBILIZED	CASUALTIES
ALLIED POWERS	42,188,810	22,104,209
CENTRAL POWERS	22,850,000	15,404,477

ALLIES
52.3% CASUALTIES

CENTRAL POWERS
67.4% CASUALTIES

© Copyright HAMMOND INCORPORATED, Maplewood, N.J.
Printed in U.S.A.

C

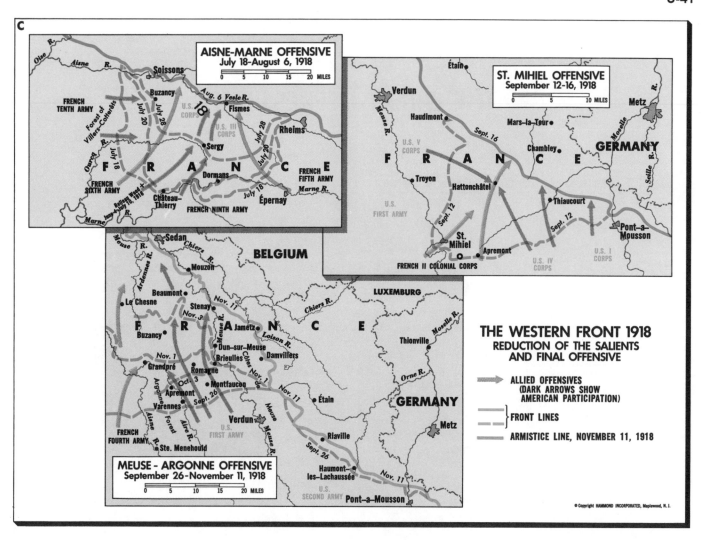

AISNE-MARNE OFFENSIVE
July 18-August 6, 1918

0   5   10   15   20 MILES

Oise R. • Aisne R. • Soissons • FRENCH TENTH ARMY • Buzancy • Forest of Villers-Cotterêts • Aug. 6 Vesle R. • Fismes • July 20 • July 28 • U.S. CORPS 18 • U.S. III CORPS • July 28 • Rheims • Sergy • July 20 • Ourcq R. • F R A N C E • Dormans • July 18 • FRENCH FIFTH ARMY • FRENCH SIXTH ARMY • Marne R. • Château-Thierry • Line Before July 18, 1918 • July 18 • Épernay • FRENCH NINTH ARMY • Marne R.

ST. MIHIEL OFFENSIVE
September 12-16, 1918

0   5   10 MILES

Étain • Verdun • Haudimont • Mars-la-Tour • Metz • Sept. 16 • Chambley • GERMANY • Moselle R. • U.S. V CORPS • F R A N C E • Troyon • Hattonchâtel • Thiaucourt • Seille R. • U.S. FIRST ARMY • Sept. 12 • Sept. 12 • St. Mihiel • Apremont • Pont-à-Mousson • FRENCH II COLONIAL CORPS • U.S. IV CORPS • U.S. I CORPS

Meuse R. • Sedan • Chiers R. • BELGIUM • Mouzon • LUXEMBURG • Ardennes R. • Beaumont • Nov. 11 • Le Chesne • Stenay • Nov. 3 • F R A N C E • Jametz • Chiers R. • Thionville • Moselle R. • Buzancy • Meuse R. • Loison R. • Dun-sur-Meuse • Damvillers • Côtes R. • Nov. 1 • Brieulles • Orne R. • Nov. 1 • Grandpré • Romagne • GERMANY • Oct. 3 • Montfaucon • Nov. 11 • Argonne Forest • Apremont • Nov. 11 • Sept. 26 • Étain • Metz • Varennes • Sept. 26 • Aisne R. • Aire R. • Verdun • Meuse R. • Riaville • FRENCH FOURTH ARMY • U.S. FIRST ARMY • Ste. Menehould • Sept. 26

MEUSE-ARGONNE OFFENSIVE
September 26-November 11, 1918

0   5   10   15   20 MILES

Haumont-les-Lachaussée • Nov. 11 • Pont-à-Mousson • U.S. SECOND ARMY

THE WESTERN FRONT 1918
REDUCTION OF THE SALIENTS
AND FINAL OFFENSIVE

➡ ALLIED OFFENSIVES
(DARK ARROWS SHOW
AMERICAN PARTICIPATION)

} FRONT LINES

ARMISTICE LINE, NOVEMBER 11, 1918

© Copyright HAMMOND INCORPORATED, Maplewood, N.J.

D

EUROPE IN THE 1920'S

PURPLE BANDS INDICATE POST-WAR BOUNDARIES
NEW COUNTRIES ARE UNDERLINED

ICELAND • NORWAY • SWEDEN • FINLAND • ESTONIA • GREAT BRITAIN • EIRE • DENMARK • LATVIA • LITHUANIA • DANZIG • NETH. • BELG. • GERMANY • POLAND • UNION OF SOVIET SOCIALIST REPUBLICS / RUSSIAN EMPIRE • LUX. • SAAR • CZECHOSLOVAKIA • FRANCE • SWITZ. • AUSTRIA-HUNGARY • PORTUGAL • SPAIN • ITALY • YUGOSLAVIA • RUMANIA • SERBIA • MONTE-NEGRO • ALB. • BULGARIA • GREECE • TURKEY / OTTOMAN EMPIRE • PERSIA • SYRIA (Fr. Mandate) • Mesopotamia • IRAQ (Br. Mandate) • KUWAIT (Br. Prot.) (Neutral Zone) • MOROCCO (Fr.) • ALGERIA (Fr.) • TUNISIA (Fr.) • (Italian) • PALESTINE (Br. Mandate) • RIO DE ORO (Sp.) • LIBYA (It.) • TRANS-JORDAN (Br. Mandate) • SAUDI ARABIA • EGYPT (Br. Prot.)

SCALE OF MILES
0   100 200 300 400 500

© Copyright HAMMOND INCORPORATED, Maplewood, N.J.

A

THE GREAT DEPRESSION

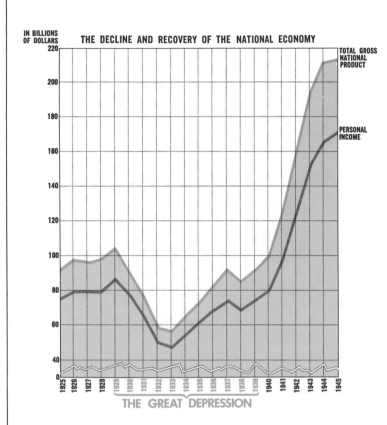

THE DECLINE AND RECOVERY OF THE NATIONAL ECONOMY

IN BILLIONS OF DOLLARS

TOTAL GROSS NATIONAL PRODUCT

PERSONAL INCOME

THE GREAT DEPRESSION

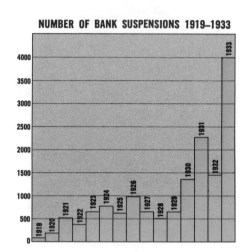

NUMBER OF BANK SUSPENSIONS 1919–1933

UNEMPLOYMENT

THE UNEMPLOYED AS A PERCENT OF THE CIVILIAN LABOR FORCE

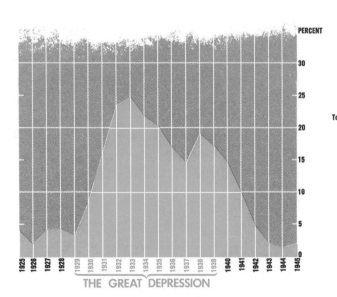

PERCENT

THE GREAT DEPRESSION

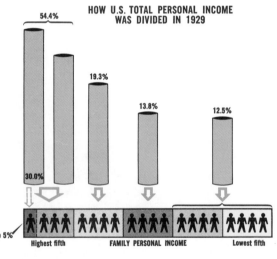

HOW U.S. TOTAL PERSONAL INCOME WAS DIVIDED IN 1929

54.4%

30.0%

19.3%

13.8%

12.5%

Top 5%

Highest fifth   FAMILY PERSONAL INCOME   Lowest fifth

HOURS

HOURS WORKED IN MANUFACTURING (1925–1945)
(WEEKLY AVERAGE)

Source: *Historical Statistics of the United States*

THE GREAT DEPRESSION
SPECULATION IN THE STOCK MARKET

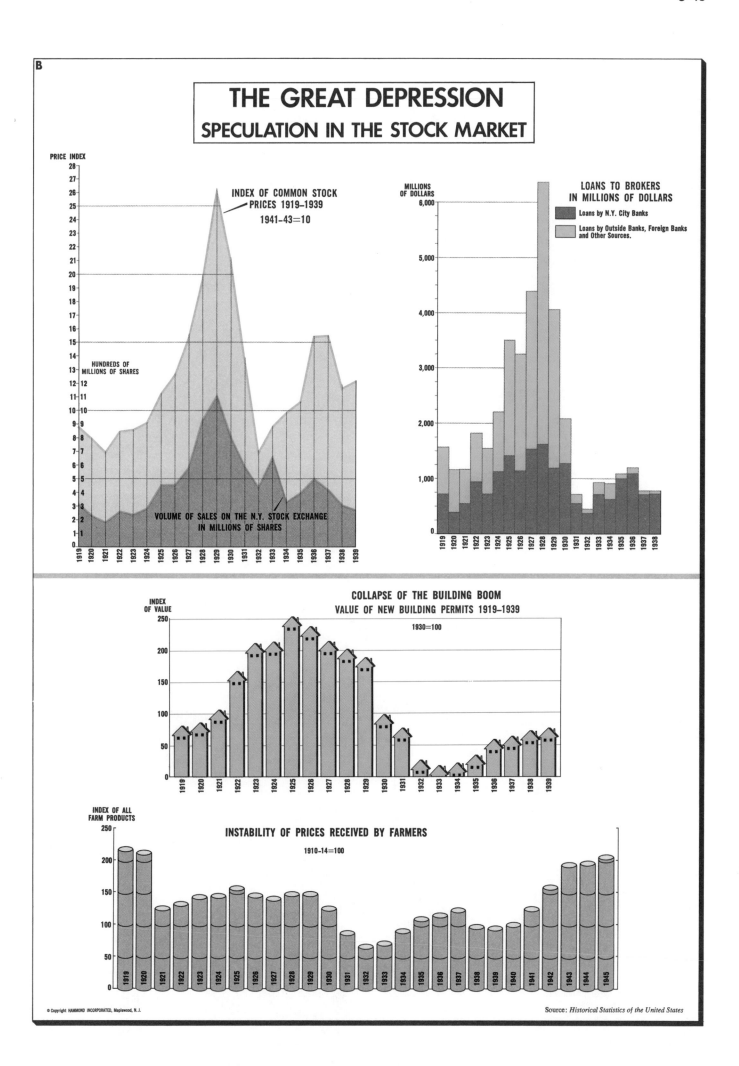

INDEX OF COMMON STOCK PRICES 1919–1939
1941–43=10

VOLUME OF SALES ON THE N.Y. STOCK EXCHANGE IN MILLIONS OF SHARES

LOANS TO BROKERS IN MILLIONS OF DOLLARS
- Loans by N.Y. City Banks
- Loans by Outside Banks, Foreign Banks and Other Sources.

COLLAPSE OF THE BUILDING BOOM
VALUE OF NEW BUILDING PERMITS 1919–1939
1930=100

INSTABILITY OF PRICES RECEIVED BY FARMERS
1910–14=100

© Copyright HAMMOND INCORPORATED, Maplewood, N.J.

Source: *Historical Statistics of the United States*

A

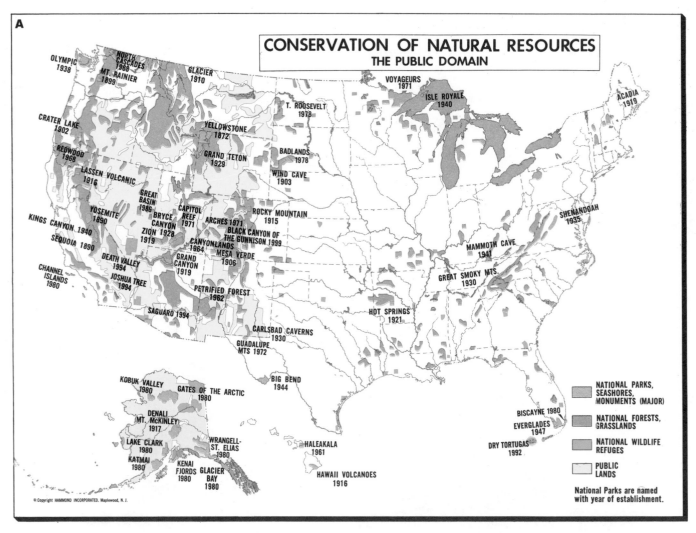

CONSERVATION OF NATURAL RESOURCES
THE PUBLIC DOMAIN

OLYMPIC 1938
NORTH CASCADES 1968
MT. RAINIER 1899
GLACIER 1910
VOYAGEURS 1971
ISLE ROYALE 1940
ACADIA 1919
CRATER LAKE 1902
T. ROOSEVELT 1978
REDWOOD 1968
YELLOWSTONE 1872
LASSEN VOLCANIC 1916
GRAND TETON 1929
BADLANDS 1978
WIND CAVE 1903
GREAT BASIN 1986
YOSEMITE 1890
BRYCE CANYON 1971
CAPITOL REEF 1971
ARCHES 1971
ROCKY MOUNTAIN 1915
SHENANDOAH 1935
KINGS CANYON 1940
ZION 1928
BLACK CANYON OF THE GUNNISON 1999
SEQUOIA 1890
CANYONLANDS 1964
MESA VERDE 1906
MAMMOTH CAVE 1941
DEATH VALLEY 1994
GRAND CANYON 1919
CHANNEL ISLANDS 1980
JOSHUA TREE 1994
GREAT SMOKY MTS. 1930
PETRIFIED FOREST 1962
SAGUARO 1994
HOT SPRINGS 1921
CARLSBAD CAVERNS 1930
GUADALUPE MTS 1972
KOBUK VALLEY 1980
GATES OF THE ARCTIC 1980
BIG BEND 1944
BISCAYNE 1980
EVERGLADES 1947
DENALI (MT. McKINLEY) 1917
LAKE CLARK 1980
WRANGELL-ST. ELIAS 1980
DRY TORTUGAS 1992
KATMAI 1980
KENAI FJORDS 1980
GLACIER BAY 1980
HALEAKALA 1961
HAWAII VOLCANOES 1916

© Copyright HAMMOND INCORPORATED, Maplewood, N.J.

Legend:
- NATIONAL PARKS, SEASHORES, MONUMENTS (MAJOR)
- NATIONAL FORESTS, GRASSLANDS
- NATIONAL WILDLIFE REFUGES
- PUBLIC LANDS

National Parks are named with year of establishment.

B

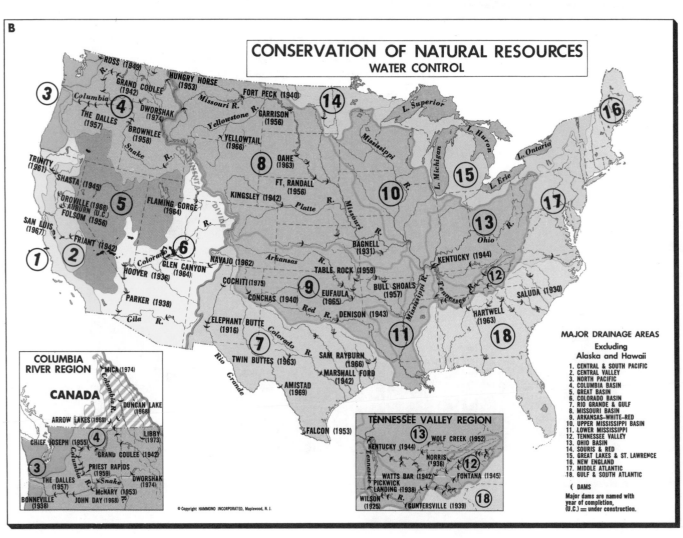

CONSERVATION OF NATURAL RESOURCES
WATER CONTROL

ROSS (1949)
GRAND COULEE (1942)
HUNGRY HORSE (1953)
FORT PECK (1940)
DWORSHAK (1974)
THE DALLES (1957)
GARRISON (1956)
BROWNLEE (1958)
YELLOWTAIL (1966)
TRINITY (1961)
OAHE (1963)
SHASTA (1945)
FT. RANDALL (1956)
OROVILLE (1968)
AUBURN (U.C.)
FLAMING GORGE (1964)
KINGSLEY (1942)
FOLSOM (1956)
SAN LUIS (1967)
FRIANT (1942)
BAGNELL (1931)
NAVAJO (1962)
GLEN CANYON (1964)
TABLE ROCK (1959)
KENTUCKY (1944)
HOOVER (1936)
COCHITI (1975)
EUFAULA (1965)
BULL SHOALS (1957)
PARKER (1938)
CONCHAS (1940)
DENISON (1943)
SALUDA (1930)
ELEPHANT BUTTE (1916)
HARTWELL (1963)
TWIN BUTTES (1963)
SAM RAYBURN (1966)
MARSHALL FORD (1942)
AMISTAD (1969)
FALCON (1953)

COLUMBIA RIVER REGION
MICA (1974)
CANADA
DUNCAN LAKE (1968)
ARROW LAKES (1969)
LIBBY (1973)
CHIEF JOSEPH (1955)
GRAND COULEE (1942)
PRIEST RAPIDS (1959)
DWORSHAK (1974)
THE DALLES (1957)
McNARY (1953)
BONNEVILLE (1938)
JOHN DAY (1968)

TENNESSEE VALLEY REGION
KENTUCKY (1944)
WOLF CREEK (1952)
NORRIS (1936)
WATTS BAR (1942)
FONTANA (1945)
PICKWICK LANDING (1938)
WILSON (1925)
GUNTERSVILLE (1939)

© Copyright HAMMOND INCORPORATED, Maplewood, N.J.

MAJOR DRAINAGE AREAS
Excluding Alaska and Hawaii

1. CENTRAL & SOUTH PACIFIC
2. CENTRAL VALLEY
3. NORTH PACIFIC
4. COLUMBIA BASIN
5. GREAT BASIN
6. COLORADO BASIN
7. RIO GRANDE & GULF
8. MISSOURI BASIN
9. ARKANSAS-WHITE-RED
10. UPPER MISSISSIPPI BASIN
11. LOWER MISSISSIPPI
12. TENNESSEE VALLEY
13. OHIO BASIN
14. SOURIS & RED
15. GREAT LAKES & ST. LAWRENCE
16. NEW ENGLAND
17. MIDDLE ATLANTIC
18. GULF & SOUTH ATLANTIC

⦅ DAMS

Major dams are named with year of completion.
(U.C.) = under construction.

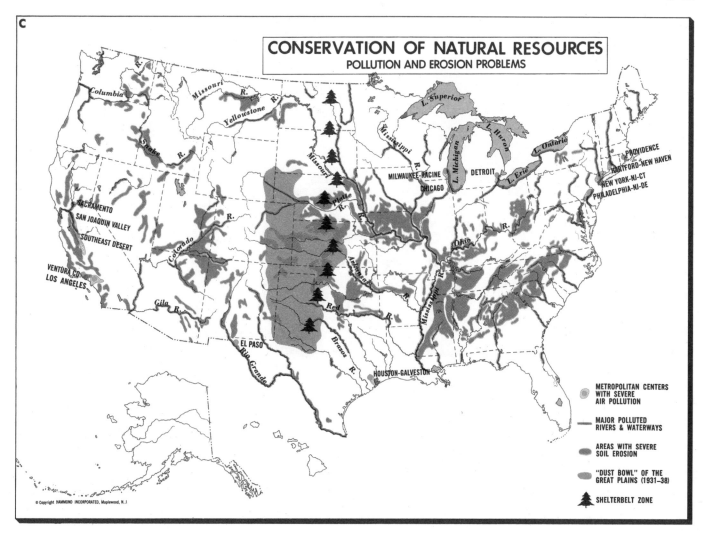

CONSERVATION OF NATURAL RESOURCES
POLLUTION AND EROSION PROBLEMS

© Copyright HAMMOND INCORPORATED, Maplewood, N.J.

- ⬤ METROPOLITAN CENTERS WITH SEVERE AIR POLLUTION
- ━ MAJOR POLLUTED RIVERS & WATERWAYS
- ▬ AREAS WITH SEVERE SOIL EROSION
- ▬ "DUST BOWL" OF THE GREAT PLAINS (1931–38)
- 🌲 SHELTERBELT ZONE

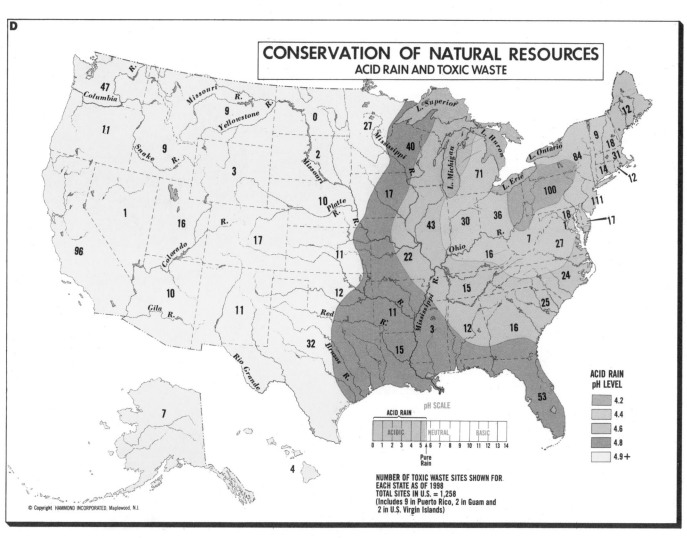

CONSERVATION OF NATURAL RESOURCES
ACID RAIN AND TOXIC WASTE

© Copyright HAMMOND INCORPORATED, Maplewood, N.J.

ACID RAIN pH LEVEL

- 4.2
- 4.4
- 4.6
- 4.8
- 4.9+

pH SCALE

ACID RAIN

ACIDIC — NEUTRAL — BASIC

0 1 2 3 4 5 6 7 8 9 10 11 12 13 14

Pure Rain

NUMBER OF TOXIC WASTE SITES SHOWN FOR EACH STATE AS OF 1998
TOTAL SITES IN U.S. = 1,258
(Includes 9 in Puerto Rico, 2 in Guam and 2 in U.S. Virgin Islands)

A

GERMAN EXPANSION 1935-1939*

SCALE OF MILES

0   100   200   300   400

Germany 1933

Area gained by Plebiscite 1935

Areas annexed 1938

Area annexed 1939

German Protectorates

*To Invasion of Poland Sept. 1, 1939

© Copyright HAMMOND INCORPORATED, Maplewood, N. J.

Map A labels:
- NORWAY, SWEDEN, FINLAND
- UNITED KINGDOM, GREAT BRITAIN, IRELAND, NO. IRELAND
- NORTH SEA, BALTIC SEA
- DENMARK
- ESTONIA, LATVIA, LITHUANIA
- MEMEL To Germany 1939
- DANZIG, East Prussia, Polish Corridor
- POLAND
- NETHERLANDS, BELGIUM, LUX.
- Rhineland remilitarized 1936
- Berlin
- GERMANY
- BOHEMIA & MORAVIA German Protectorate and occupation 1939
- SAAR To Germany 1935
- SUDETENLAND To Germany 1938
- Sudetenland, BOHEMIA & MORAVIA, CZECHOSLOVAKIA, SLOVAKIA
- To Hung. 1939
- SLOVAKIA German Protectorate 1939
- Munich, AUSTRIA
- AUSTRIA To Germany 1938
- SWITZ.
- HUNGARY
- RUMANIA
- FRANCE
- ATLANTIC OCEAN
- ITALY, ADRIATIC SEA
- YUGOSLAVIA
- Danube, BLACK SEA
- BULGARIA
- PORTUGAL, SPAIN, Civil War 1936-1939
- MEDITERRANEAN SEA
- ALBANIA (To Italy 1939)
- GREECE, TURKEY
- UNION OF SOVIET SOCIALIST REPUBLICS

B

WORLD WAR II 1939-1940*

SCALE OF MILES

0   100   200   300   400

Germany and Slovakia

Allied Nations

Neutral Nations

Areas occupied by Germany

Areas occupied by U.S.S.R.

⟹ German Advances

⟹ British Advances

⟹ Russian Advances

*To July 1, 1940

International Boundaries Sept. 1, 1939

© Copyright HAMMOND INCORPORATED, Maplewood, N. J.

Map B labels:
- NORWAY, SWEDEN, FINLAND
- RUSSO-FINNISH WAR 1939-1940
- NORTH SEA, BALTIC SEA
- UNITED KINGDOM, GREAT BRITAIN, IRELAND, NO. IRELAND
- London
- DENMARK
- German invasion of Norway and Denmark April 9, 1940
- German invasion of Low Countries May 10, 1940
- ESTONIA, LATVIA, LITHUANIA
- Estonia, Latvia and Lithuania annexed by U.S.S.R. 1940
- DANZIG, East Prussia
- Berlin
- GERMANY
- Warsaw
- POLAND
- U.S.S.R. invasion of Poland September 17, 1939
- German invasion of Poland September 1, 1939 Start of World War II
- NETHERLANDS, BELGIUM, LUX.
- Dunkirk
- Battle of France May-June 1940
- Paris
- MAGINOT LINE
- Vichy Government established July 1940
- FRANCE, Vichy
- SWITZ.
- Austria
- HUNGARY
- SLOVAKIA
- Partition of Poland September 27, 1939
- Bessarabia and northern Bukovina annexed by U.S.S.R. 1940
- Bessarabia
- RUMANIA
- Italy declares war on Great Britain and France June 1940
- ATLANTIC OCEAN
- ITALY, ADRIATIC SEA
- YUGOSLAVIA
- Danube, BLACK SEA
- BULGARIA
- PORTUGAL, SPAIN
- MEDITERRANEAN SEA
- ALBANIA (Italy)
- GREECE, TURKEY
- U.S.S.R.

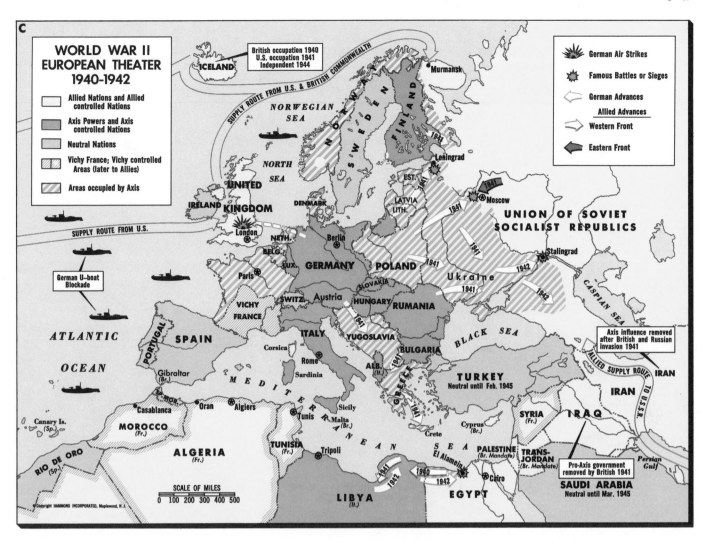

C

WORLD WAR II EUROPEAN THEATER 1940-1942

Allied Nations and Allied controlled Nations

Axis Powers and Axis controlled Nations

Neutral Nations

Vichy France; Vichy controlled Areas (later to Allies)

Areas occupied by Axis

German Air Strikes

Famous Battles or Sieges

German Advances

Allied Advances

Western Front

Eastern Front

British occupation 1940 U.S. occupation 1941 Independent 1944

ICELAND

SUPPLY ROUTE FROM U.S. & BRITISH COMMONWEALTH

NORWEGIAN SEA

NORTH SEA

SWEDEN

NORWAY

FINLAND

Murmansk

Leningrad

EST.

LATVIA LITH.

Moscow

UNION OF SOVIET SOCIALIST REPUBLICS

SUPPLY ROUTE FROM U.S.

UNITED KINGDOM

IRELAND

DENMARK

London

NETH.

BELG.

LUX.

Berlin

GERMANY

POLAND

Ukraine

Stalingrad

German U-boat Blockade

Paris

SWITZ.

Austria

HUNGARY

SLOVAKIA

RUMANIA

CASPIAN SEA

VICHY FRANCE

ATLANTIC

OCEAN

PORTUGAL

SPAIN

Corsica

Rome

Sardinia

ITALY

YUGOSLAVIA

ALB. (It.)

BULGARIA

GREECE

BLACK SEA

TURKEY Neutral until Feb. 1945

Axis influence removed after British and Russian invasion 1941

IRAN

ALLIED SUPPLY ROUTE TO U.S.S.R.

IRAN

Gibraltar (Br.)

MOR.

Canary Is. (Sp.)

Casablanca

Oran

Algiers

MEDITERRANEAN

Tunis

Malta (Br.)

Sicily

Crete

SEA

Cyprus (Br.)

SYRIA (Fr.)

IRAQ

MOROCCO (Fr.)

RIO DE ORO (Sp.)

ALGERIA (Fr.)

TUNISIA (Fr.)

Tripoli

LIBYA (It.)

El Alamein

EGYPT

Cairo

PALESTINE (Br. Mandate)

TRANS-JORDAN (Br. Mandate)

Persian Gulf

Pro-Axis government removed by British 1941

SAUDI ARABIA Neutral until Mar. 1945

SCALE OF MILES
0 100 200 300 400 500

©Copyright HAMMOND INCORPORATED, Maplewood, N.J.

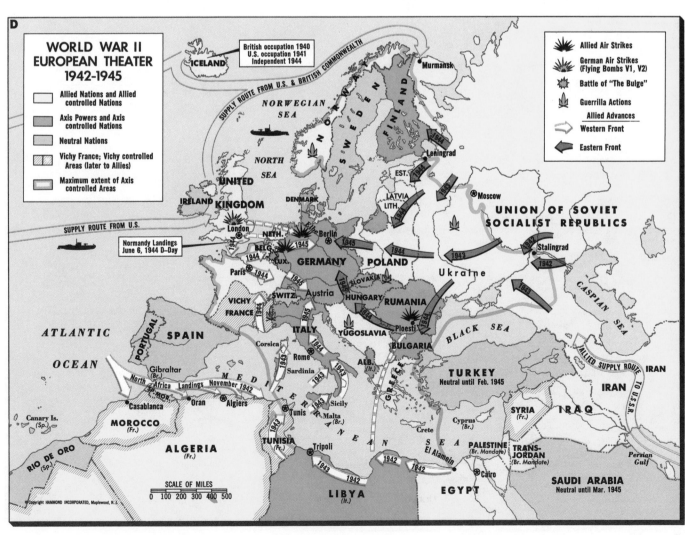

D

WORLD WAR II EUROPEAN THEATER 1942-1945

Allied Nations and Allied controlled Nations

Axis Powers and Axis controlled Nations

Neutral Nations

Vichy France; Vichy controlled Areas (later to Allies)

Maximum extent of Axis controlled Areas

Allied Air Strikes

German Air Strikes (Flying Bombs V1, V2)

Battle of "The Bulge"

Guerrilla Actions

Allied Advances

Western Front

Eastern Front

British occupation 1940 U.S. occupation 1941 Independent 1944

ICELAND

SUPPLY ROUTE FROM U.S. & BRITISH COMMONWEALTH

NORWEGIAN SEA

NORTH SEA

SWEDEN

NORWAY

FINLAND

Murmansk

Leningrad

EST.

LATVIA LITH.

Moscow

UNION OF SOVIET SOCIALIST REPUBLICS

SUPPLY ROUTE FROM U.S.

UNITED KINGDOM

IRELAND

DENMARK

London

Normandy Landings June 6, 1944 D-Day

NETH.

BELG.

LUX.

Berlin

GERMANY

POLAND

Ukraine

Stalingrad

Paris

SWITZ.

Austria

SLOVAKIA

HUNGARY

RUMANIA

Ploesti

CASPIAN SEA

VICHY FRANCE

ATLANTIC

OCEAN

PORTUGAL

SPAIN

Corsica

Rome

Sardinia

ITALY

YUGOSLAVIA

ALB. (It.)

BULGARIA

GREECE

BLACK SEA

TURKEY Neutral until Feb. 1945

IRAN

ALLIED SUPPLY ROUTE TO U.S.S.R.

IRAN

Gibraltar (Br.)

North Africa Landings November 1942

MOR.

Canary Is. (Sp.)

Casablanca

Oran

Algiers

MEDITERRANEAN

Tunis

Malta (Br.)

Sicily

Crete

SEA

Cyprus (Br.)

SYRIA (Fr.)

IRAQ

MOROCCO (Fr.)

RIO DE ORO (Sp.)

ALGERIA (Fr.)

TUNISIA (Fr.)

Tripoli

LIBYA (It.)

El Alamein

EGYPT

Cairo

PALESTINE (Br. Mandate)

TRANS-JORDAN (Br. Mandate)

Persian Gulf

SAUDI ARABIA Neutral until Mar. 1945

SCALE OF MILES
0 100 200 300 400 500

©Copyright HAMMOND INCORPORATED, Maplewood, N.J.

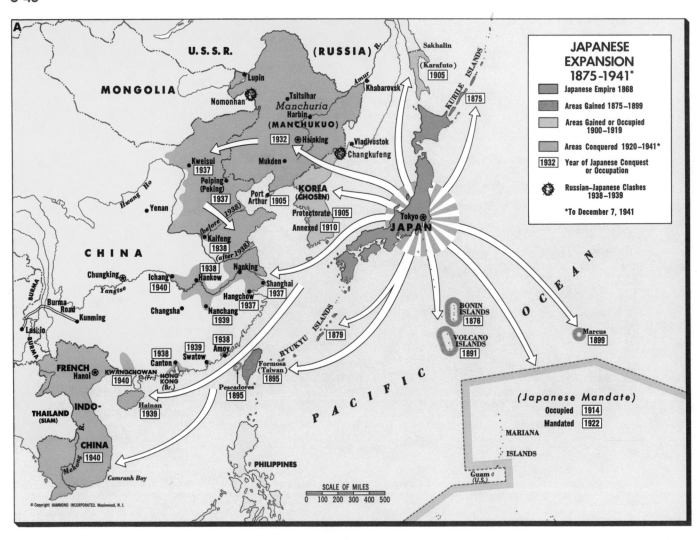

A

JAPANESE EXPANSION 1875-1941*

Japanese Empire 1868
Areas Gained 1875-1899
Areas Gained or Occupied 1900-1919
Areas Conquered 1920-1941*
1932 — Year of Japanese Conquest or Occupation
⊕ — Russian–Japanese Clashes 1938-1939

*To December 7, 1941

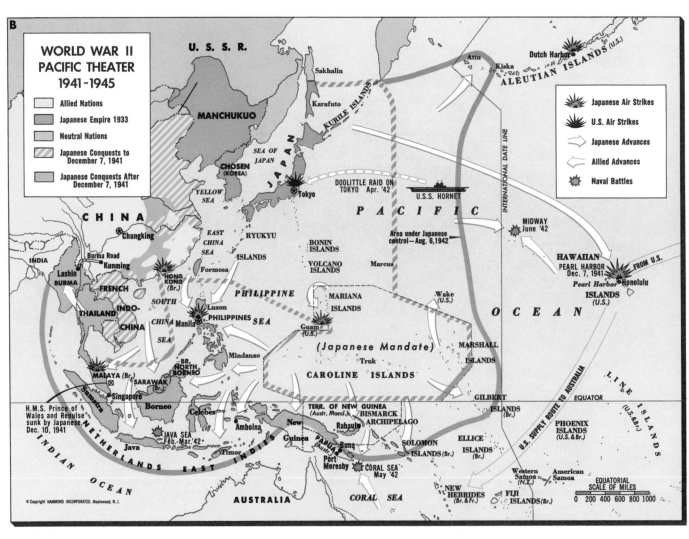

B

WORLD WAR II PACIFIC THEATER 1941-1945

Allied Nations
Japanese Empire 1933
Neutral Nations
Japanese Conquests to December 7, 1941
Japanese Conquests After December 7, 1941

Japanese Air Strikes
U.S. Air Strikes
Japanese Advances
Allied Advances
Naval Battles

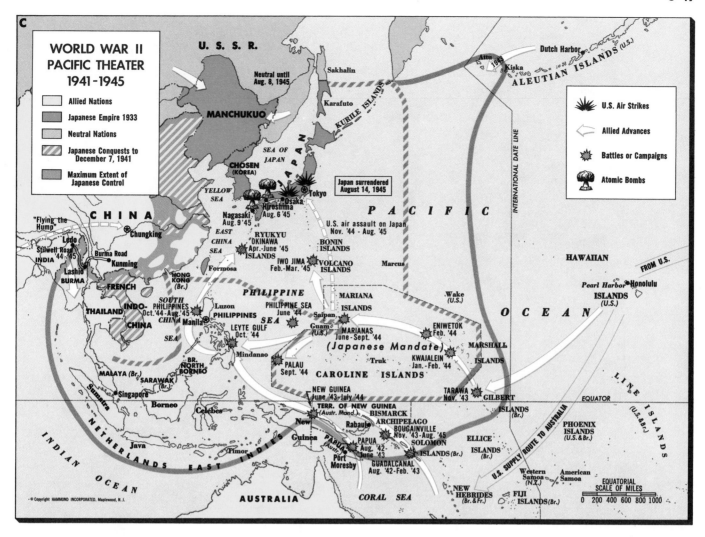

C

WORLD WAR II PACIFIC THEATER 1941-1945

Allied Nations
Japanese Empire 1933
Neutral Nations
Japanese Conquests to December 7, 1941
Maximum Extent of Japanese Control

U.S. Air Strikes
Allied Advances
Battles or Campaigns
Atomic Bombs

U.S.S.R.

Neutral until Aug. 8, 1945

Sakhalin

Karafuto

MANCHUKUO

KURILE ISLANDS

Attu 1943
Kiska
Dutch Harbor (U.S.)
ALEUTIAN ISLANDS (U.S.)

SEA OF JAPAN

CHOSEN (KOREA)

CHINA

"Flying the Hump"

Ledo
Stilwell Road '44 '45
INDIA
Burma Road
Lashio
BURMA
Kunming
FRENCH
INDO-CHINA
THAILAND

Chungking

YELLOW SEA

Nagasaki Aug. 9 '45
RYUKYU OKINAWA Apr.-June '45 ISLANDS
Formosa

EAST CHINA SEA

Hiroshima Aug. 6 '45
Osaka

Tokyo

Japan surrendered August 14, 1945

PACIFIC

U.S. air assault on Japan Nov. '44 - Aug. '45

HAWAIIAN

FROM U.S.

Pearl Harbor Honolulu
ISLANDS (U.S.)

OCEAN

HONG KONG (Br.)

PHILIPPINE

SOUTH PHILIPPINES Oct.'44-Aug.'45

Luzon
Manila
PHILIPPINES
LEYTE GULF Oct. '44

PHILIPPINE SEA June '44

CHINA SEA

Mindanao

IWO JIMA Feb.-Mar. '45
BONIN ISLANDS
VOLCANO ISLANDS

Marcus

MARIANA ISLANDS

Saipan
Guam (U.S.)

MARIANAS June-Sept. '44

Wake (U.S.)

ENIWETOK Feb. '44

MARSHALL ISLANDS

KWAJALEIN Jan.-Feb. '44

LINE

EQUATOR

ISLANDS (U.S. & Br.)

MALAYA (Br.)
BR. NORTH BORNEO
SARAWAK (Br.)
Singapore

PALAU Sept. '44

(Japanese Mandate)

Truk

CAROLINE ISLANDS

TARAWA Nov. '43
GILBERT

ISLANDS (Br.)

U.S. SUPPLY ROUTE TO AUSTRALIA

PHOENIX ISLANDS (U.S. & Br.)

Sumatra

Borneo
Celebes

NETHERLANDS EAST INDIES

Java
Timor

NEW GUINEA June '43-July '44
TERR. OF NEW GUINEA (Austr. Mand.)
New Guinea
PAPUA (Austr.)
Port Moresby

BISMARCK ARCHIPELAGO
Rabaul
BOUGAINVILLE Nov. '43-Aug. '45
PAPUA Aug. '42-June '43
SOLOMON
GUADALCANAL Aug. '42-Feb. '43

ELLICE ISLANDS (Br.)
ISLANDS (Br.)

Western Samoa (N.Z.)
American Samoa

INDIAN OCEAN

AUSTRALIA

CORAL SEA

NEW HEBRIDES (Br. & Fr.)

FIJI ISLANDS (Br.)

EQUATORIAL SCALE OF MILES
0 200 400 600 800 1000

- © Copyright HAMMOND INCORPORATED, Maplewood, N.J.

INTERNATIONAL DATE LINE

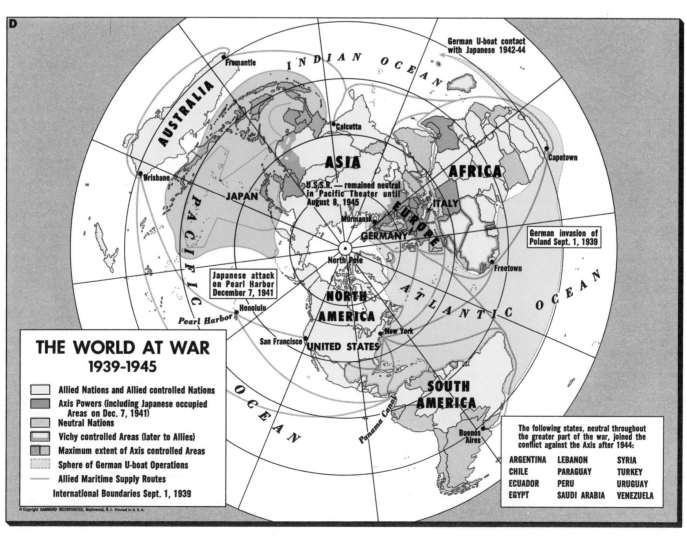

D

German U-boat contact with Japanese 1942-44

INDIAN OCEAN

AUSTRALIA

Fremantle

Calcutta

ASIA

AFRICA

Capetown

Brisbane

JAPAN

PACIFIC

U.S.S.R. — remained neutral in Pacific Theater until August 8, 1945

ITALY

EUROPE

Murmansk
GERMANY

German invasion of Poland Sept. 1, 1939

North Pole

Freetown

Japanese attack on Pearl Harbor December 7, 1941

NORTH AMERICA

ATLANTIC OCEAN

Pearl Harbor
Honolulu

San Francisco
UNITED STATES

New York

THE WORLD AT WAR 1939-1945

Allied Nations and Allied controlled Nations
Axis Powers (including Japanese occupied Areas on Dec. 7, 1941)
Neutral Nations
Vichy controlled Areas (later to Allies)
Maximum extent of Axis controlled Areas
Sphere of German U-boat Operations
Allied Maritime Supply Routes
International Boundaries Sept. 1, 1939

SOUTH AMERICA

Panama Canal

Buenos Aires

The following states, neutral throughout the greater part of the war, joined the conflict against the Axis after 1944:

ARGENTINA	LEBANON	SYRIA
CHILE	PARAGUAY	TURKEY
ECUADOR	PERU	URUGUAY
EGYPT	SAUDI ARABIA	VENEZUELA

© Copyright HAMMOND INCORPORATED, Maplewood, N.J. Printed in U.S.A.

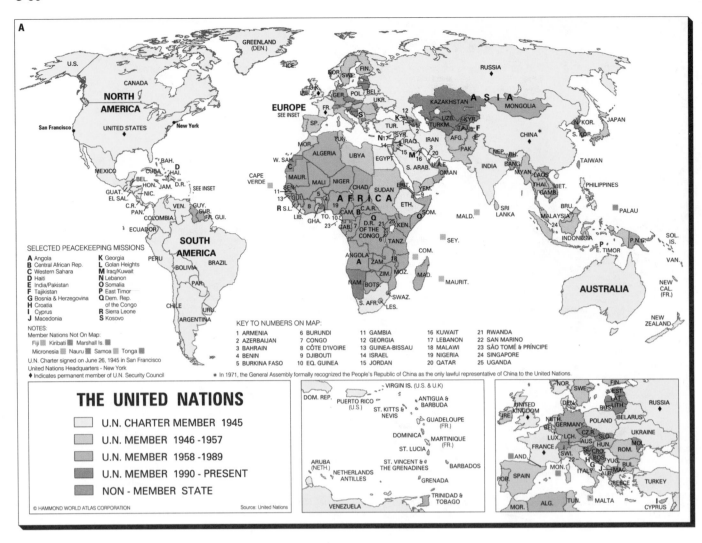

A

SELECTED PEACEKEEPING MISSIONS

A Angola
B Central African Rep.
C Western Sahara
D Haiti
E India/Pakistan
F Tajikistan
G Bosnia & Herzegovina
H Croatia
I Cyprus
J Macedonia
K Georgia
L Golan Heights
M Iraq/Kuwait
N Lebanon
O Somalia
P East Timor
Q Dem. Rep.
  of the Congo
R Sierra Leone
S Kosovo

NOTES:
Member Nations Not On Map:
Fiji Kiribati Marshall Is.
Micronesia Nauru Samoa Tonga
U.N. Charter signed on June 26, 1945 in San Francisco
United Nations Headquarters - New York
♦ Indicates permanent member of U.N. Security Council

KEY TO NUMBERS ON MAP:

1 ARMENIA	6 BURUNDI	11 GAMBIA	16 KUWAIT	21 RWANDA
2 AZERBAIJAN	7 CONGO	12 GEORGIA	17 LEBANON	22 SAN MARINO
3 BAHRAIN	8 CÔTE D'IVOIRE	13 GUINEA-BISSAU	18 MALAWI	23 SÃO TOMÉ & PRÍNCIPE
4 BENIN	9 DJIBOUTI	14 ISRAEL	19 NIGERIA	24 SINGAPORE
5 BURKINA FASO	10 EQ. GUINEA	15 JORDAN	20 QATAR	25 UGANDA

* In 1971, the General Assembly formally recognized the People's Republic of China as the only lawful representative of China to the United Nations.

THE UNITED NATIONS

- U.N. CHARTER MEMBER 1945
- U.N. MEMBER 1946 - 1957
- U.N. MEMBER 1958 - 1989
- U.N. MEMBER 1990 - PRESENT
- NON - MEMBER STATE

© HAMMOND WORLD ATLAS CORPORATION

Source: United Nations

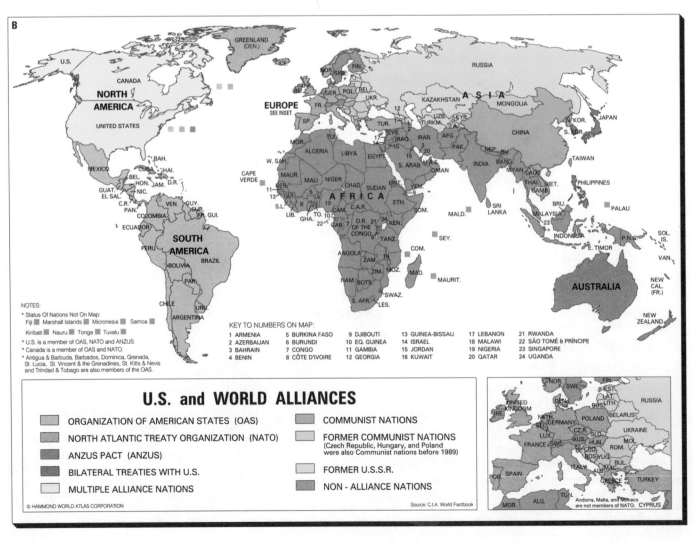

B

NOTES:

* Status Of Nations Not On Map:
Fiji Marshall Islands Micronesia Samoa
Kiribati Nauru Tonga Tuvalu

* U.S. is a member of OAS, NATO and ANZUS.
* Canada is a member of OAS and NATO.
* Antigua & Barbuda, Barbados, Dominica, Grenada,
St. Lucia, St. Vincent & the Grenadines, St. Kitts & Nevis
and Trindad & Tobago are also members of the OAS.

KEY TO NUMBERS ON MAP:

1 ARMENIA	5 BURKINA FASO	9 DJIBOUTI	13 GUINEA-BISSAU	17 LEBANON	21 RWANDA
2 AZERBAIJAN	6 BURUNDI	10 EQ. GUINEA	14 ISRAEL	18 MALAWI	22 SÃO TOMÉ & PRÍNCIPE
3 BAHRAIN	7 CONGO	11 GAMBIA	15 JORDAN	19 NIGERIA	23 SINGAPORE
4 BENIN	8 CÔTE D'IVOIRE	12 GEORGIA	16 KUWAIT	20 QATAR	24 UGANDA

U.S. and WORLD ALLIANCES

- ORGANIZATION OF AMERICAN STATES (OAS)
- NORTH ATLANTIC TREATY ORGANIZATION (NATO)
- ANZUS PACT (ANZUS)
- BILATERAL TREATIES WITH U.S.
- MULTIPLE ALLIANCE NATIONS
- COMMUNIST NATIONS
- FORMER COMMUNIST NATIONS
  (Czech Republic, Hungary, and Poland
  were also Communist nations before 1989)
- FORMER U.S.S.R.
- NON - ALLIANCE NATIONS

© HAMMOND WORLD ATLAS CORPORATION

Source: C.I.A. World Factbook

Andorra, Malta, and Monaco are not members of NATO.

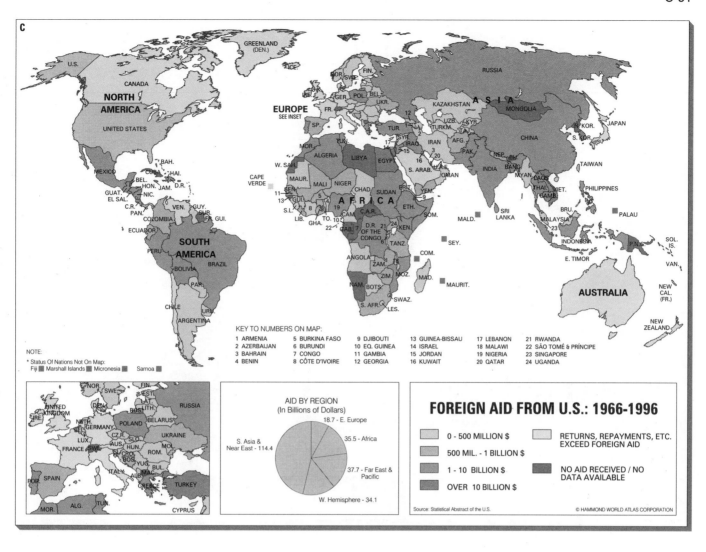

C

KEY TO NUMBERS ON MAP:

1 ARMENIA	5 BURKINA FASO	9 DJIBOUTI	13 GUINEA-BISSAU	17 LEBANON	21 RWANDA
2 AZERBAIJAN	6 BURUNDI	10 EQ. GUINEA	14 ISRAEL	18 MALAWI	22 SÃO TOMÉ & PRÍNCIPE
3 BAHRAIN	7 CONGO	11 GAMBIA	15 JORDAN	19 NIGERIA	23 SINGAPORE
4 BENIN	8 CÔTE D'IVOIRE	12 GEORGIA	16 KUWAIT	20 QATAR	24 UGANDA

NOTE:
* Status Of Nations Not On Map:
Fiji   Marshall Islands   Micronesia   Samoa

AID BY REGION
(In Billions of Dollars)

18.7 - E. Europe
35.5 - Africa
S. Asia & Near East - 114.4
37.7 - Far East & Pacific
W. Hemisphere - 34.1

FOREIGN AID FROM U.S.: 1966-1996

0 - 500 MILLION $
500 MIL. - 1 BILLION $
1 - 10 BILLION $
OVER 10 BILLION $

RETURNS, REPAYMENTS, ETC. EXCEED FOREIGN AID
NO AID RECEIVED / NO DATA AVAILABLE

Source: Statistical Abstract of the U.S.

© HAMMOND WORLD ATLAS CORPORATION

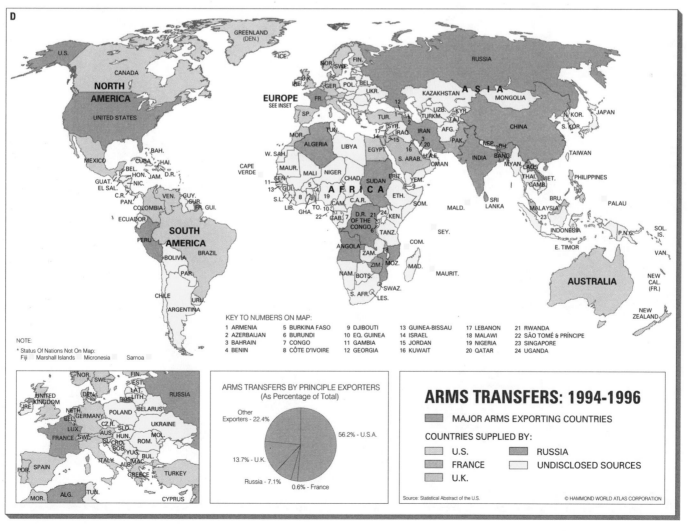

D

KEY TO NUMBERS ON MAP:

1 ARMENIA	5 BURKINA FASO	9 DJIBOUTI	13 GUINEA-BISSAU	17 LEBANON	21 RWANDA
2 AZERBAIJAN	6 BURUNDI	10 EQ. GUINEA	14 ISRAEL	18 MALAWI	22 SÃO TOMÉ & PRÍNCIPE
3 BAHRAIN	7 CONGO	11 GAMBIA	15 JORDAN	19 NIGERIA	23 SINGAPORE
4 BENIN	8 CÔTE D'IVOIRE	12 GEORGIA	16 KUWAIT	20 QATAR	24 UGANDA

NOTE:
* Status Of Nations Not On Map:
Fiji   Marshall Islands   Micronesia   Samoa

ARMS TRANSFERS BY PRINCIPLE EXPORTERS
(As Percentage of Total)

Other Exporters - 22.4%
56.2% - U.S.A.
13.7% - U.K.
Russia - 7.1%
0.6% - France

ARMS TRANSFERS: 1994-1996

MAJOR ARMS EXPORTING COUNTRIES

COUNTRIES SUPPLIED BY:
U.S.
FRANCE
U.K.
RUSSIA
UNDISCLOSED SOURCES

Source: Statistical Abstract of the U.S.

© HAMMOND WORLD ATLAS CORPORATION

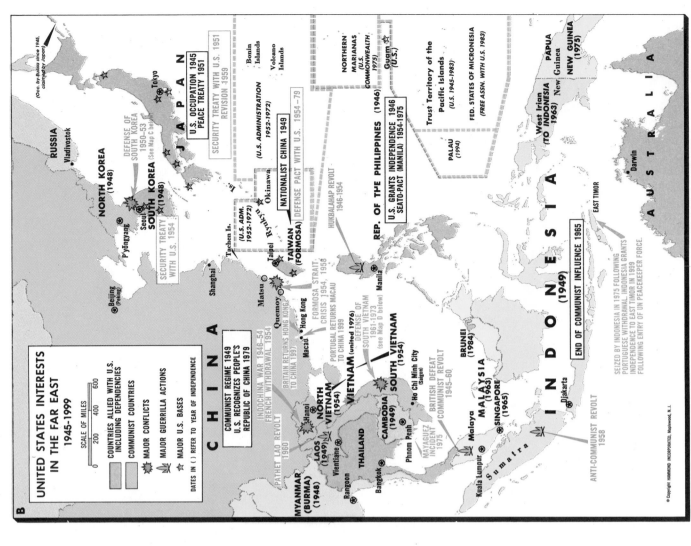

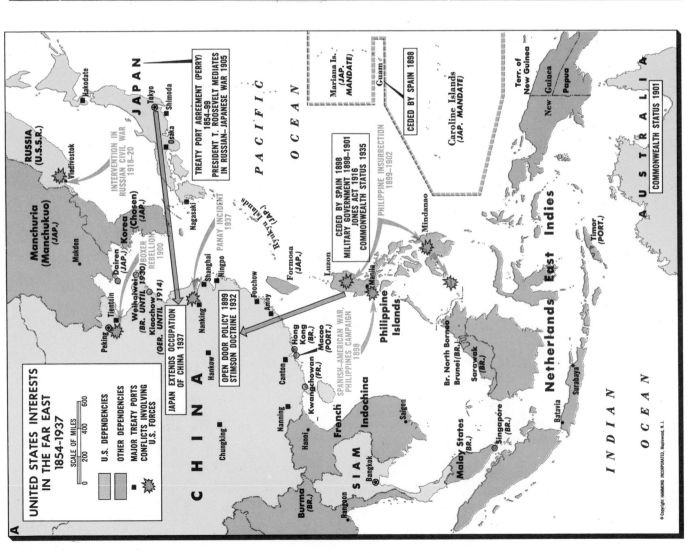

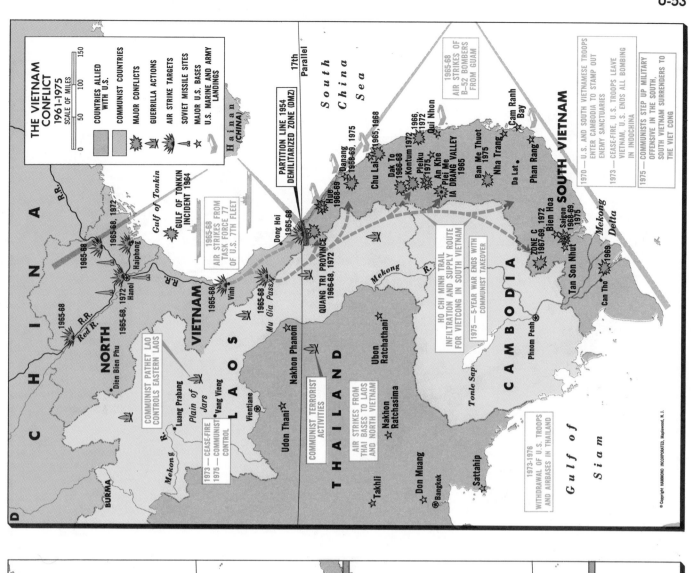

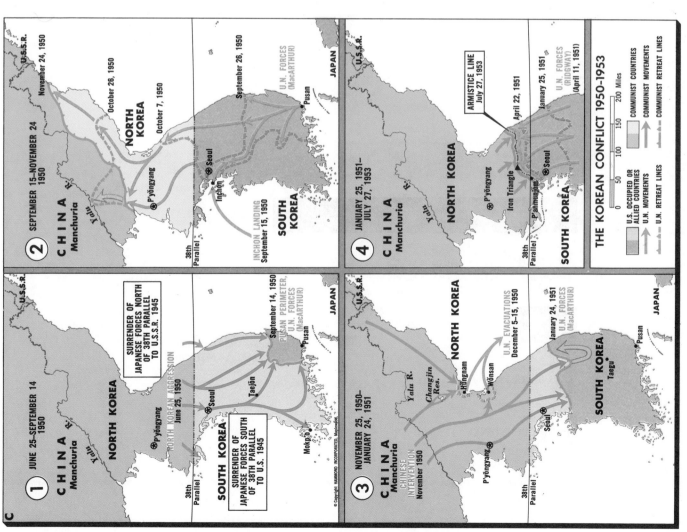

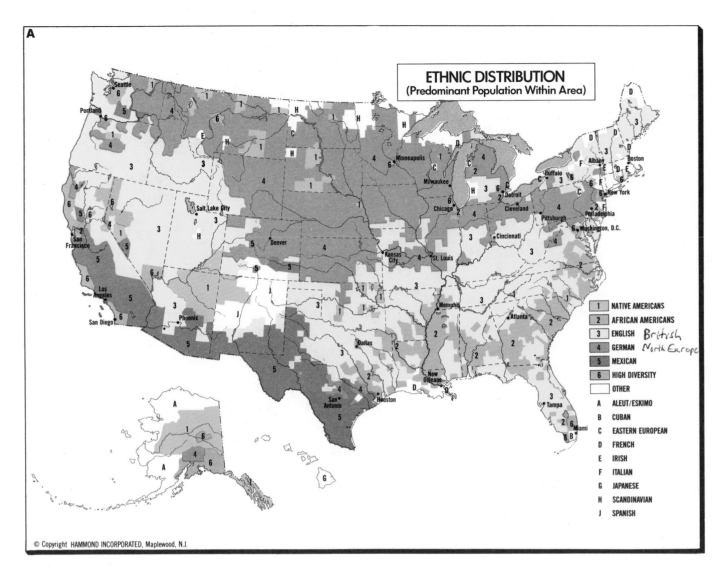

A

ETHNIC DISTRIBUTION
(Predominant Population Within Area)

1	NATIVE AMERICANS
2	AFRICAN AMERICANS
3	ENGLISH *British*
4	GERMAN *North Europe*
5	MEXICAN
6	HIGH DIVERSITY
	OTHER
A	ALEUT/ESKIMO
B	CUBAN
C	EASTERN EUROPEAN
D	FRENCH
E	IRISH
F	ITALIAN
G	JAPANESE
H	SCANDINAVIAN
J	SPANISH

© Copyright HAMMOND INCORPORATED, Maplewood, N.J.

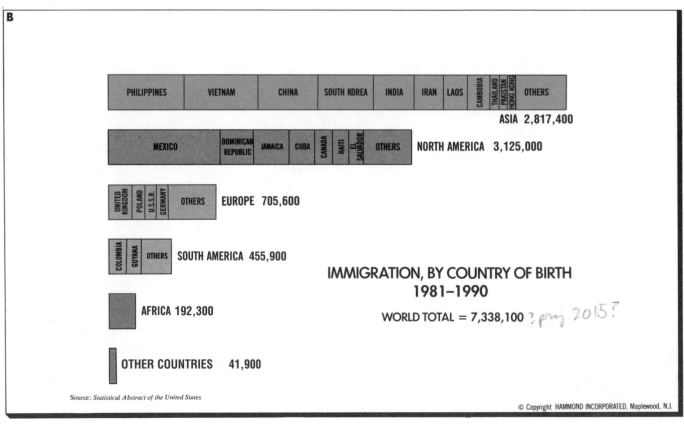

B

IMMIGRATION, BY COUNTRY OF BIRTH
1981–1990

WORLD TOTAL = 7,338,100 *? proj. 2015?*

ASIA 2,817,400 — PHILIPPINES, VIETNAM, CHINA, SOUTH KOREA, INDIA, IRAN, LAOS, CAMBODIA, THAILAND, PAKISTAN, HONG KONG, OTHERS

NORTH AMERICA 3,125,000 — MEXICO, DOMINICAN REPUBLIC, JAMAICA, CUBA, CANADA, HAITI, EL SALVADOR, OTHERS

EUROPE 705,600 — UNITED KINGDOM, POLAND, U.S.S.R., GERMANY, OTHERS

SOUTH AMERICA 455,900 — COLOMBIA, GUYANA, OTHERS

AFRICA 192,300

OTHER COUNTRIES 41,900

Source: *Statistical Abstract of the United States*

© Copyright HAMMOND INCORPORATED, Maplewood, N.J.

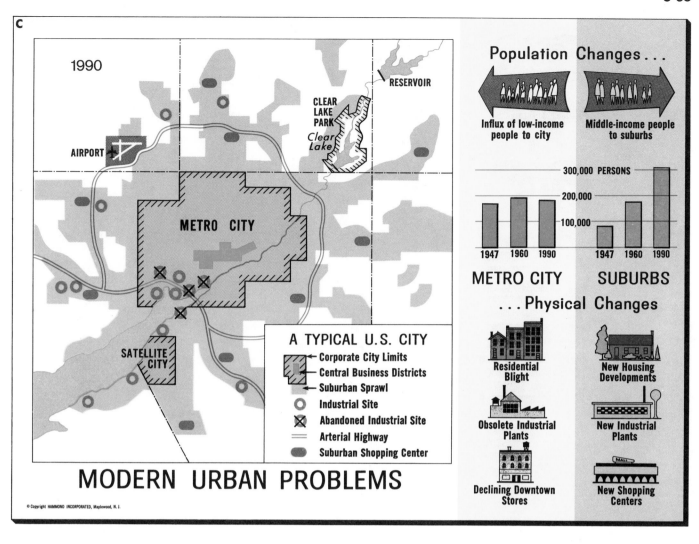

C

1990

RESERVOIR

CLEAR LAKE PARK

Clear Lake

AIRPORT

METRO CITY

SATELLITE CITY

A TYPICAL U.S. CITY

← Corporate City Limits
← Central Business Districts
← Suburban Sprawl
○ Industrial Site
✕ Abandoned Industrial Site
═ Arterial Highway
⬭ Suburban Shopping Center

MODERN URBAN PROBLEMS

© Copyright HAMMOND INCORPORATED, Maplewood, N.J.

Population Changes...

Influx of low-income people to city

Middle-income people to suburbs

300,000 PERSONS
200,000
100,000

| 1947 | 1960 | 1990 | 1947 | 1960 | 1990 |

METRO CITY   **SUBURBS**

...Physical Changes

Residential Blight

New Housing Developments

Obsolete Industrial Plants

New Industrial Plants

Declining Downtown Stores

New Shopping Centers

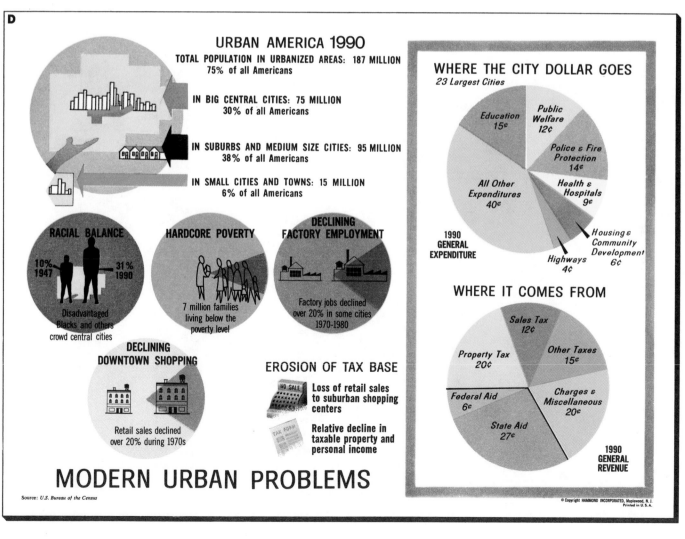

D

URBAN AMERICA 1990

TOTAL POPULATION IN URBANIZED AREAS: 187 MILLION
75% of all Americans

IN BIG CENTRAL CITIES: 75 MILLION
30% of all Americans

IN SUBURBS AND MEDIUM SIZE CITIES: 95 MILLION
38% of all Americans

IN SMALL CITIES AND TOWNS: 15 MILLION
6% of all Americans

RACIAL BALANCE
10% 1947   31% 1990
Disadvantaged Blacks and others crowd central cities

HARDCORE POVERTY
7 million families living below the poverty level

DECLINING FACTORY EMPLOYMENT
Factory jobs declined over 20% in some cities 1970-1980

DECLINING DOWNTOWN SHOPPING
Retail sales declined over 20% during 1970s

EROSION OF TAX BASE
Loss of retail sales to suburban shopping centers

Relative decline in taxable property and personal income

MODERN URBAN PROBLEMS

Source: *U.S. Bureau of the Census*

WHERE THE CITY DOLLAR GOES
23 Largest Cities

Education 15¢
Public Welfare 12¢
Police & Fire Protection 14¢
Health & Hospitals 9¢
All Other Expenditures 40¢
Housing & Community Development 6¢
Highways 4¢

1990 GENERAL EXPENDITURE

WHERE IT COMES FROM

Sales Tax 12¢
Property Tax 20¢
Other Taxes 15¢
Federal Aid 6¢
Charges & Miscellaneous 20¢
State Aid 27¢

1990 GENERAL REVENUE

© Copyright HAMMOND INCORPORATED, Maplewood, N.J.
Printed in U.S.A.

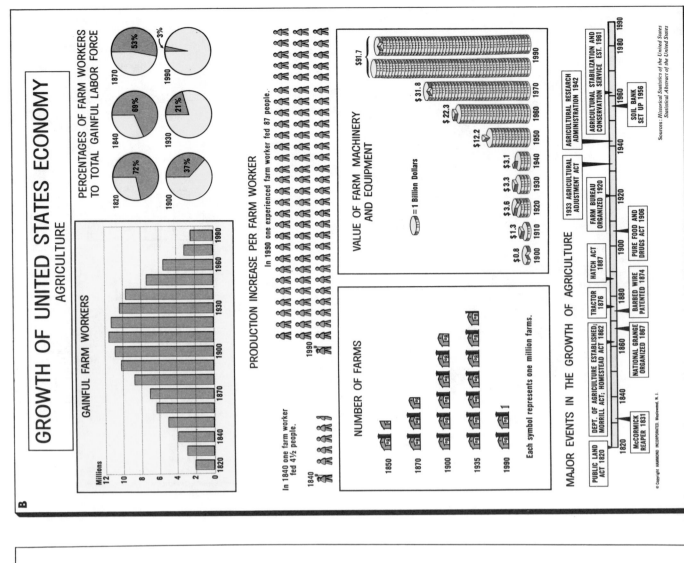

GROWTH OF UNITED STATES ECONOMY
AGRICULTURE

PERCENTAGES OF FARM WORKERS TO TOTAL GAINFUL LABOR FORCE

1820 72% — 1840 69% — 1870 53%
1900 37% — 1930 21% — 1990 ~3%

GAINFUL FARM WORKERS

Millions
12 10 8 6 4 2 0
1820 1840 1870 1900 1930 1960 1990

PRODUCTION INCREASE PER FARM WORKER

In 1840 one farm worker fed 4½ people.
1840

In 1990 one experienced farm worker fed 87 people.
1990

NUMBER OF FARMS

1850
1870
1900
1935
1990

Each symbol represents one million farms.

VALUE OF FARM MACHINERY AND EQUIPMENT

= 1 Billion Dollars

$0.8 — 1900
$1.3 — 1910
$3.6 — 1920
$3.3 — 1930
$3.1 — 1940
$12.2 — 1950
$22.3 — 1960
$31.8 — 1970
$91.7 — 1990

MAJOR EVENTS IN THE GROWTH OF AGRICULTURE

PUBLIC LAND ACT 1820
DEPT. OF AGRICULTURE ESTABLISHED; MORRILL ACT; HOMESTEAD ACT 1862
McCORMICK REAPER 1831
NATIONAL GRANGE ORGANIZED 1867
TRACTOR 1876
BARBED WIRE PATENTED 1874
HATCH ACT 1887
PURE FOOD AND DRUGS ACT 1906
FARM BUREAU ORGANIZED 1920
1933 AGRICULTURAL ADJUSTMENT ACT
AGRICULTURAL RESEARCH ADMINISTRATION 1942
AGRICULTURAL STABILIZATION AND CONSERVATION SERVICE EST. 1961
SOIL BANK SET UP 1956

1820 1840 1860 1880 1900 1920 1940 1960 1980 1990

Sources: Historical Statistics of the United States
Statistical Abstract of the United States

B

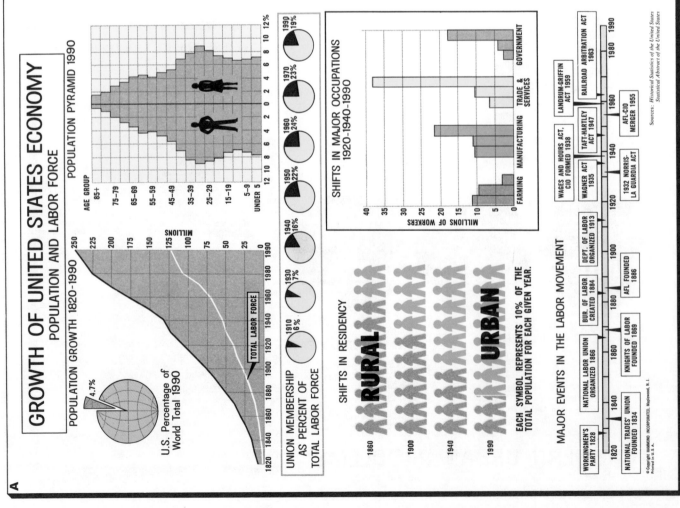

GROWTH OF UNITED STATES ECONOMY
POPULATION AND LABOR FORCE

POPULATION GROWTH 1820-1990

MILLIONS
250 225 200 175 150 125 100 75 50 25 0
1820 1840 1860 1880 1900 1920 1940 1960 1980 1990

TOTAL LABOR FORCE

U.S. Percentage of World Total 1990
4.7%

POPULATION PYRAMID 1990

AGE GROUP
85+
75–79
65–69
55–59
45–49
35–39
25–29
15–19
5–9
UNDER 5

12 10 8 6 4 2 0 2 4 6 8 10 12%

UNION MEMBERSHIP AS PERCENT OF TOTAL LABOR FORCE

1910 6% — 1930 7% — 1940 16% — 1950 22% — 1960 24% — 1970 23% — 1990 19%

SHIFTS IN MAJOR OCCUPATIONS 1920-1940-1990

MILLIONS OF WORKERS
40 35 30 25 20 15 10 5 0
FARMING   MANUFACTURING   TRADE & SERVICES   GOVERNMENT

SHIFTS IN RESIDENCY

RURAL
1860
1900
1940
1990

URBAN

EACH SYMBOL REPRESENTS 10% OF THE TOTAL POPULATION FOR EACH GIVEN YEAR.

MAJOR EVENTS IN THE LABOR MOVEMENT

WORKINGMEN'S PARTY 1828
NATIONAL TRADES' UNION FOUNDED 1834
NATIONAL LABOR UNION ORGANIZED 1866
KNIGHTS OF LABOR FOUNDED 1869
BUR. OF LABOR CREATED 1884
AFL FOUNDED 1886
DEPT. OF LABOR ORGANIZED 1913
1932 NORRIS-LA GUARDIA ACT
WAGNER ACT 1935
WAGES AND HOURS ACT, CIO FORMED 1938
TAFT-HARTLEY ACT 1947
AFL-CIO MERGER 1955
LANDRUM-GRIFFIN ACT 1959
RAILROAD ARBITRATION ACT 1963

1820 1840 1860 1880 1900 1920 1940 1960 1980 1990

Sources: Historical Statistics of the United States
Statistical Abstract of the United States

A

D

GROWTH OF UNITED STATES ECONOMY
NATIONAL PRODUCT AND INCOME

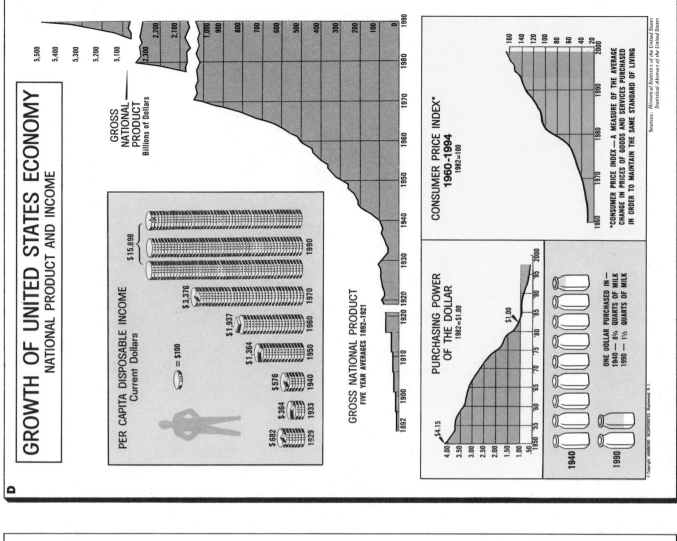

GROSS
NATIONAL
PRODUCT
Billions of Dollars

PER CAPITA DISPOSABLE INCOME
Current Dollars

= $100

$15,898
$3,376
$1,937
$1,364
$576
$364
$682

1990
1970
1960
1950
1940
1933
1929

GROSS NATIONAL PRODUCT
FIVE YEAR AVERAGES 1892–1921

CONSUMER PRICE INDEX*
1960–1994
1982=100

PURCHASING POWER
OF THE DOLLAR
1982=$1.00

$4.15
$1.00

ONE DOLLAR PURCHASED IN—
1940 — 8¾ QUARTS OF MILK
1990 — 1⅓ QUARTS OF MILK

1940
1990

*CONSUMER PRICE INDEX—A MEASURE OF THE AVERAGE
CHANGE IN PRICES OF GOODS AND SERVICES PURCHASED
IN ORDER TO MAINTAIN THE SAME STANDARD OF LIVING

Sources: *Historical Statistics of the United States*
Statistical Abstract of the United States

© Copyright HAMMOND INCORPORATED, Maplewood, N.J.

C

GROWTH OF UNITED STATES ECONOMY
TRANSPORTATION

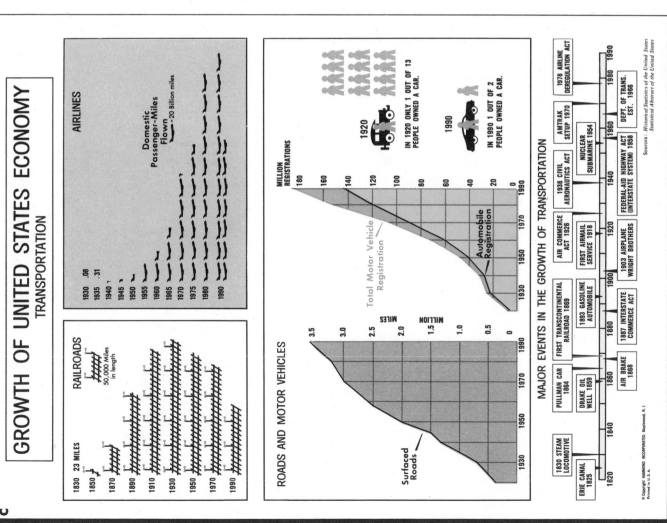

AIRLINES

Domestic
Passenger-Miles
Flown
20 Billion miles

1930 .08
1935 .31
1940
1945
1950
1955
1960
1965
1970
1975
1980
1990

RAILROADS
50,000 Miles
in length

1830 23 MILES
1850
1870
1890
1910
1930
1950
1970
1990

ROADS AND MOTOR VEHICLES

MILLION
REGISTRATIONS

Total Motor Vehicle
Registration

Automobile
Registration

Surfaced
Roads

MILLION
MILES

1920
1990

IN 1920 ONLY 1 OUT OF 13
PEOPLE OWNED A CAR.

IN 1990 1 OUT OF 2
PEOPLE OWNED A CAR.

MAJOR EVENTS IN THE GROWTH OF TRANSPORTATION

ERIE CANAL
1825
1830 STEAM
LOCOMOTIVE
AIR BRAKE
1868
DRAKE OIL
WELL 1859
PULLMAN CAR
1864
FIRST TRANSCONTINENTAL
RAILROAD 1869
1887 INTERSTATE
COMMERCE ACT
1893 GASOLINE
AUTOMOBILE
1903 AIRPLANE
WRIGHT BROTHERS
FIRST AIRMAIL
SERVICE 1918
AIR COMMERCE ACT 1926
1938 CIVIL
AERONAUTICS ACT
NUCLEAR
SUBMARINE 1954
FEDERAL-AID HIGHWAY ACT
(INTERSTATE SYSTEM) 1958
AMTRAK
SETUP 1970
DEPT. OF TRANS.
EST. 1966
1978 AIRLINE
DEREGULATION ACT

1820
1840
1860
1880
1900
1920
1940
1960
1980
1990

Sources: *Historical Statistics of the United States*
Statistical Abstract of the United States

© Copyright HAMMOND INCORPORATED, Maplewood, N.J.
Printed in U.S.A.

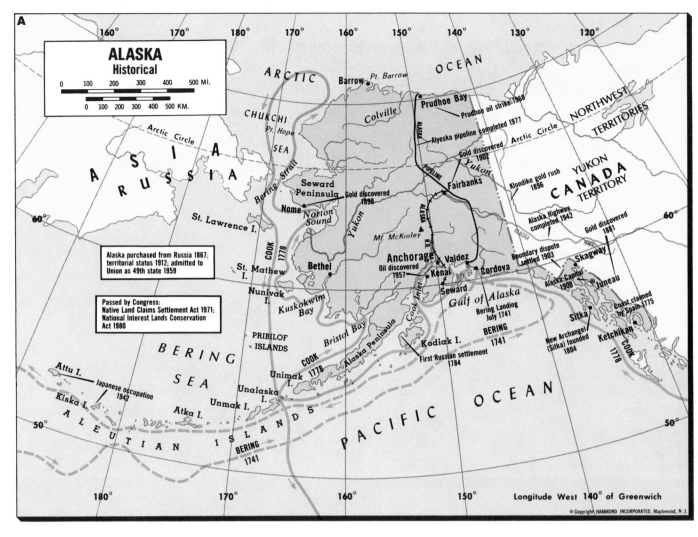

A

ALASKA
Historical

0 100 200 300 400 500 MI.
0 100 200 300 400 500 KM.

ARCTIC   OCEAN

Barrow • Pt. Barrow

Prudhoe Bay
Prudhoe oil strike 1968

NORTHWEST
TERRITORIES

CHUKCHI
Pt. Hope

Colville

ALASKA

Alyeska pipeline completed 1977   Arctic Circle

Gold discovered
1902

YUKON

CANADA

TERRITORY

Arctic Circle

SEA

Bering Strait

Seward
Peninsula
Gold discovered
1899

Fairbanks

Klondike gold rush
1896

Yukon

RUSSIA

ASIA

St. Lawrence I.

Nome
Norton
Sound

PIPELINE

Alaska Highway
completed 1942

Gold discovered
1881

60°

60°

COOK
1778

Yukon

ALASKA R.R.

Mt. McKinley ▲

Boundary dispute
settled 1903

Skagway

Alaska purchased from Russia 1867;
territorial status 1912; admitted to
Union as 49th state 1959

St. Mathew
I.

Bethel

Anchorage
Oil discovered
1957

Valdez

Kenai

Cordova

Alaska Capital
1900

Juneau

Nunivak
I.

Seward

Coast claimed
by Spain 1775

Passed by Congress:
Native Land Claims Settlement Act 1971;
National Interest Lands Conservation
Act 1980

Kuskokwim
Bay

Cook Inlet

Gulf of Alaska

Bering Landing
July 1741

BERING

Sitka

PRIBILOF
ISLANDS

Bristol Bay

COOK
1778

Kodiak I.

1741

New Archangel
(Sitka) founded
1804

Ketchikan

COOK
1778

BERING

Unimak
I.

Alaska Peninsula

First Russian settlement
1784

SEA

Attu I.
Japanese occupation
1942

Unalaska
I.

Unmak I.

Kiska I.

Atka I.

ALEUTIAN   ISLANDS

PACIFIC   OCEAN

50°

BERING
1741

50°

Longitude West **140°** of Greenwich

© Copyright HAMMOND INCORPORATED, Maplewood, N.J.

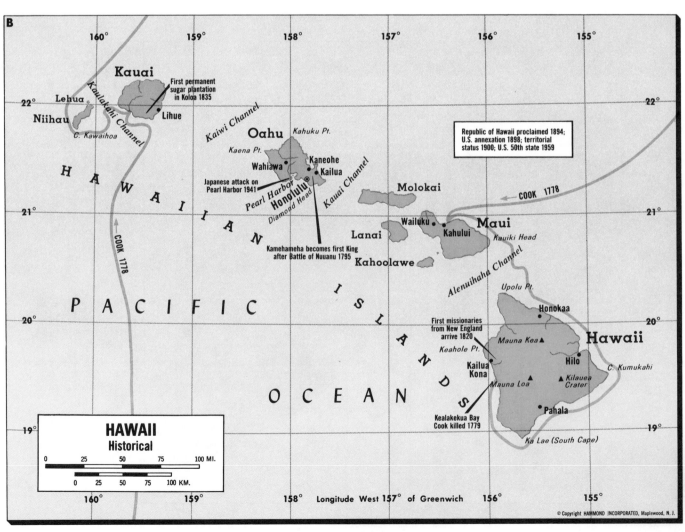

B

Kauai
First permanent
sugar plantation
in Koloa 1835

Lehua

Keälakahi Channel

Lihue

Niihau
C. Kawaihoa

Kaiwi Channel

Oahu
Kahuku Pt.

Republic of Hawaii proclaimed 1894;
U.S. annexation 1898; territorial
status 1900; U.S. 50th state 1959

22°

22°

Kaena Pt.

Wahiawa

Kaneohe
Kailua

H

Japanese attack on
Pearl Harbor 1941

Pearl Harbor
Honolulu
Diamond Head

Kauai Channel

Molokai

COOK 1778

A

Kamehameha becomes first King
after Battle of Nuuanu 1795

Lanai

Wailuku
Kahului

Maui
Kauiki Head

21°

21°

W

Kahoolawe

Alenuihaha Channel

Upolu Pt.

A

First missionaries
from New England
arrive 1820

Honokaa

I

Keahole Pt.

Mauna Kea ▲

Hawaii

Kailua
Kona

Mauna Loa ▲

Hilo

Kilauea
Crater

C. Kumukahi

20°

I

COOK
1778

N

Kealakekua Bay
Cook killed 1779

Pahala

20°

PACIFIC

A

Ka Lae (South Cape)

OCEAN

N

D

S

HAWAII
Historical

0   25   50   75   100 MI.
0   25   50   75   100 KM.

19°

19°

Longitude West **157°** of Greenwich

© Copyright HAMMOND INCORPORATED, Maplewood, N.J.

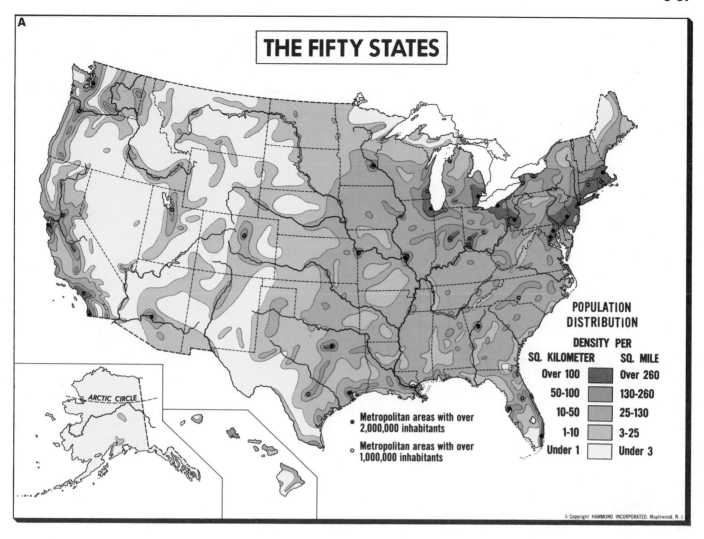

THE FIFTY STATES

POPULATION DISTRIBUTION

DENSITY PER

SQ. KILOMETER	SQ. MILE
Over 100	Over 260
50-100	130-260
10-50	25-130
1-10	3-25
Under 1	Under 3

ARCTIC CIRCLE

● Metropolitan areas with over 2,000,000 inhabitants

○ Metropolitan areas with over 1,000,000 inhabitants

© Copyright HAMMOND INCORPORATED, Maplewood, N.J.

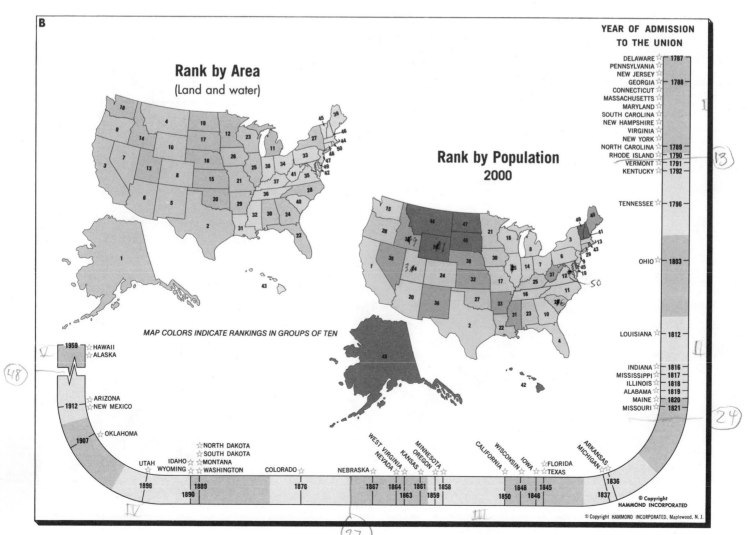

Rank by Area
(Land and water)

Rank by Population 2000

MAP COLORS INDICATE RANKINGS IN GROUPS OF TEN

YEAR OF ADMISSION TO THE UNION

DELAWARE ☆	1787
PENNSYLVANIA ☆	
NEW JERSEY ☆	
GEORGIA ☆	1788
CONNECTICUT ☆	
MASSACHUSETTS ☆	
MARYLAND ☆	
SOUTH CAROLINA ☆	
NEW HAMPSHIRE ☆	
VIRGINIA ☆	
NEW YORK ☆	
NORTH CAROLINA ☆	1789
RHODE ISLAND ☆	1790
VERMONT ☆	1791
KENTUCKY ☆	1792
TENNESSEE ☆	1796
OHIO ☆	1803
LOUISIANA ☆	1812
INDIANA ☆	1816
MISSISSIPPI ☆	1817
ILLINOIS ☆	1818
ALABAMA ☆	1819
MAINE ☆	1820
MISSOURI ☆	1821

1959 ☆ HAWAII ☆ ALASKA

1912 ☆ ARIZONA ☆ NEW MEXICO

1907 ☆ OKLAHOMA

☆ NORTH DAKOTA ☆ SOUTH DAKOTA

UTAH ☆ IDAHO ☆ MONTANA
☆ WYOMING ☆ WASHINGTON COLORADO ☆ NEBRASKA ☆ WEST VIRGINIA NEVADA ☆ KANSAS MINNESOTA OREGON ☆ CALIFORNIA WISCONSIN ☆ IOWA ☆ FLORIDA ☆ TEXAS ARKANSAS MICHIGAN

1836
1896 1889 1876 1867 1864 1861 1858 1848 1845 1837
1890 1863 1859 1850 1846

© Copyright HAMMOND INCORPORATED

© Copyright HAMMOND INCORPORATED, Maplewood, N.J.

POPULATION CHARACTERISTICS

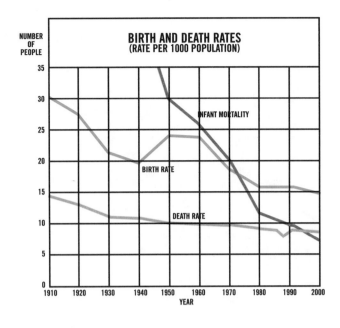

BIRTH AND DEATH RATES
(RATE PER 1000 POPULATION)

NUMBER OF PEOPLE

INFANT MORTALITY

BIRTH RATE

DEATH RATE

YEAR

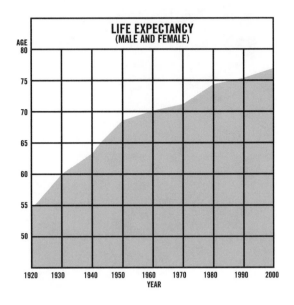

LIFE EXPECTANCY
(MALE AND FEMALE)

AGE

YEAR

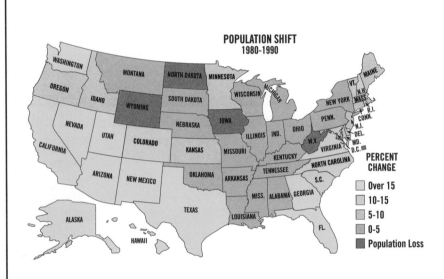

POPULATION SHIFT
1980-1990

PERCENT CHANGE

- Over 15
- 10-15
- 5-10
- 0-5
- Population Loss

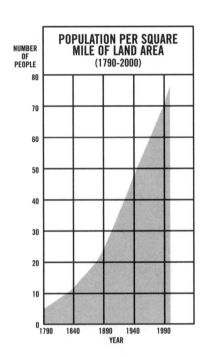

POPULATION PER SQUARE MILE OF LAND AREA
(1790-2000)

NUMBER OF PEOPLE

YEAR

POPULATION SHIFT
1990-2000

PERCENT CHANGE

- Over 15
- 10-15
- 5-10
- 0-5
- Population Loss

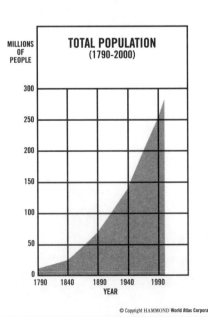

TOTAL POPULATION
(1790-2000)

MILLIONS OF PEOPLE

YEAR

Source: *Statistical Abstract of the US*

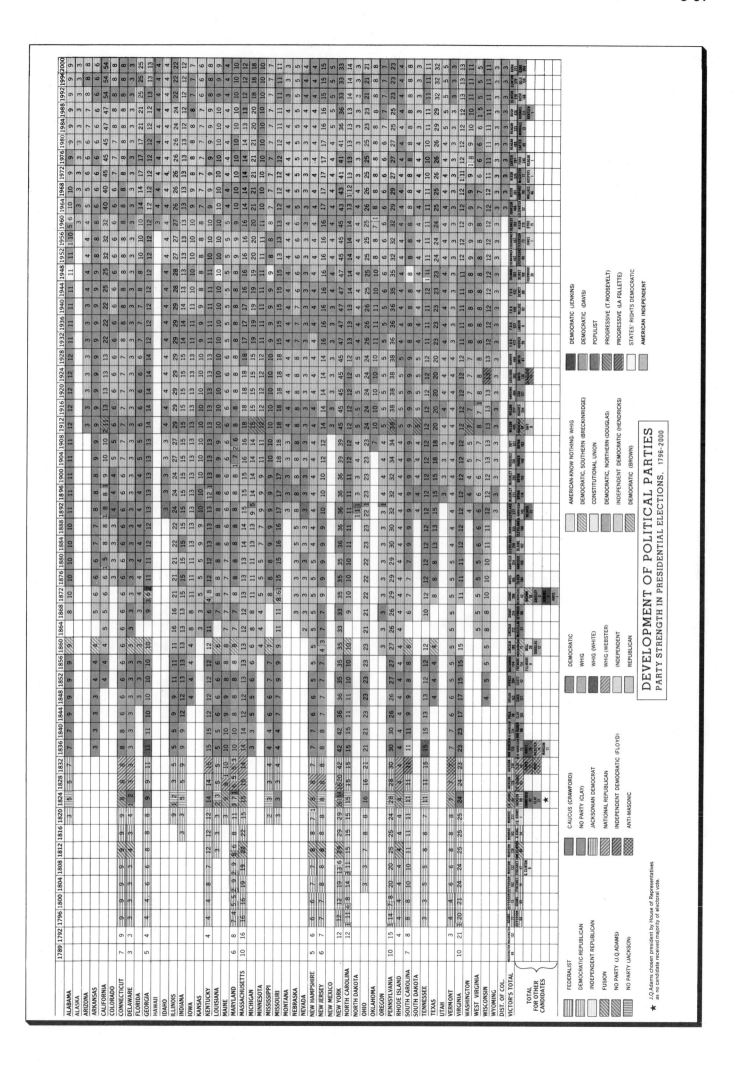

DEVELOPMENT OF POLITICAL PARTIES
PARTY STRENGTH IN PRESIDENTIAL ELECTIONS, 1796-2000

★ J.Q.Adams chosen president by House of Representatives
as no candidate received majority of electoral vote.

POLITICAL SECTIONALISM 1796-1868
PRESIDENTIAL ELECTORAL VOTE BY STATES AND PARTIES

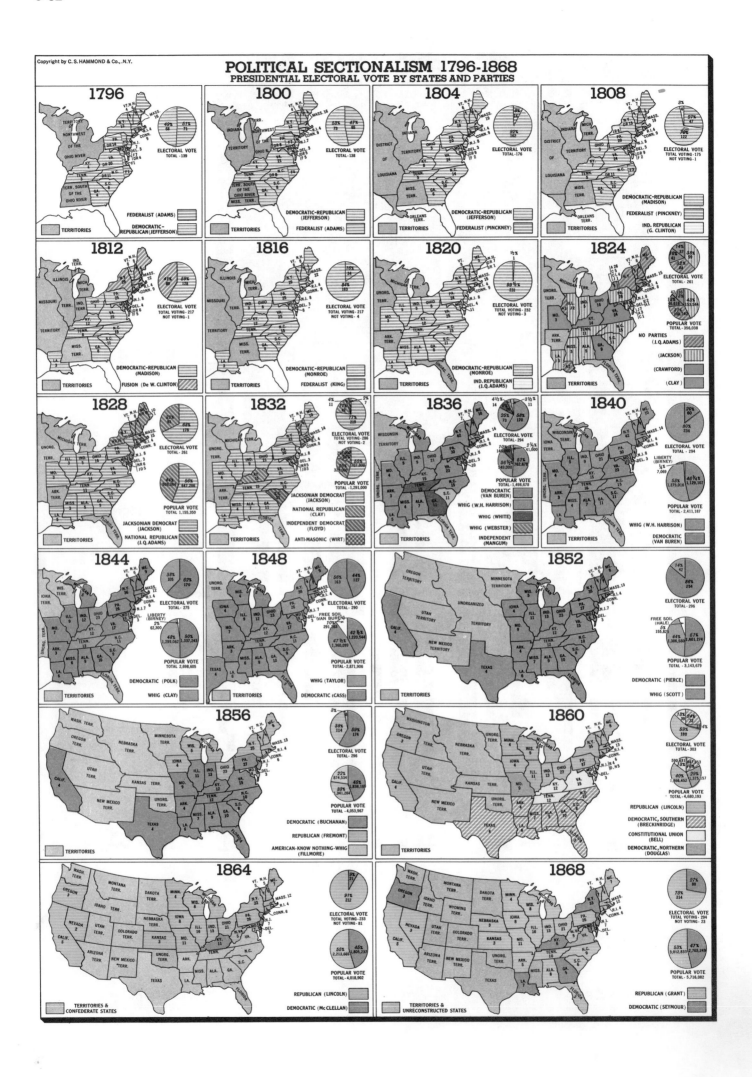

POLITICAL SECTIONALISM 1872-1916
PRESIDENTIAL ELECTORAL VOTE BY STATES AND PARTIES

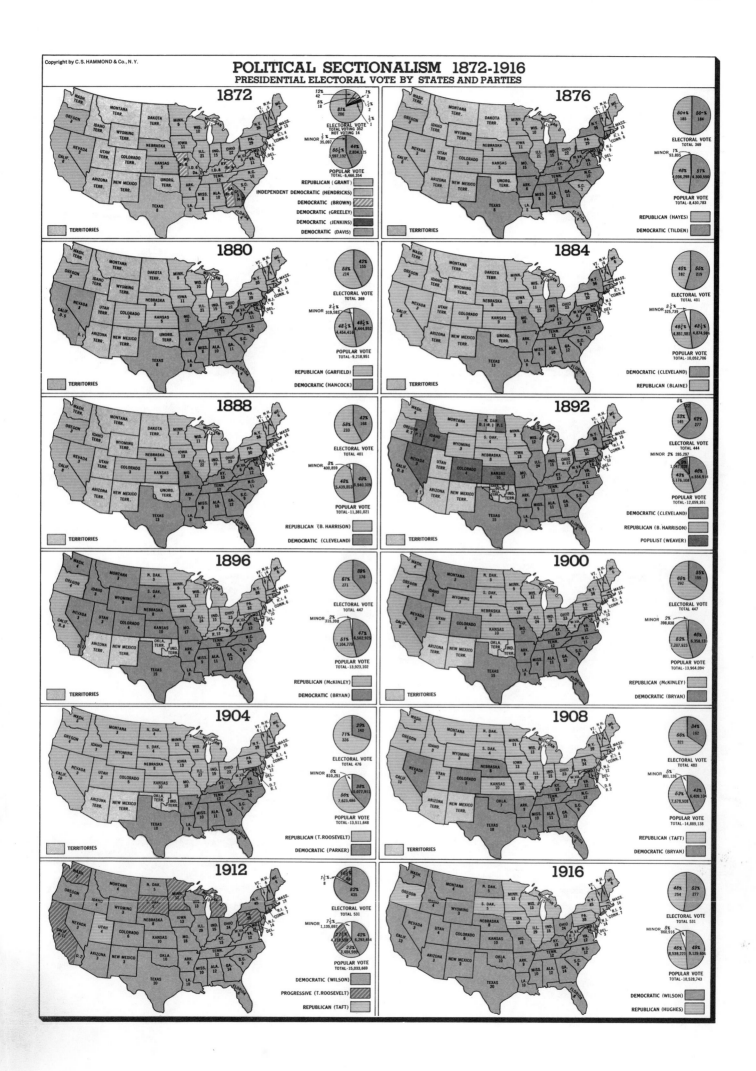

POLITICAL SECTIONALISM 1920-1964
PRESIDENTIAL ELECTORAL VOTE BY STATES AND PARTIES

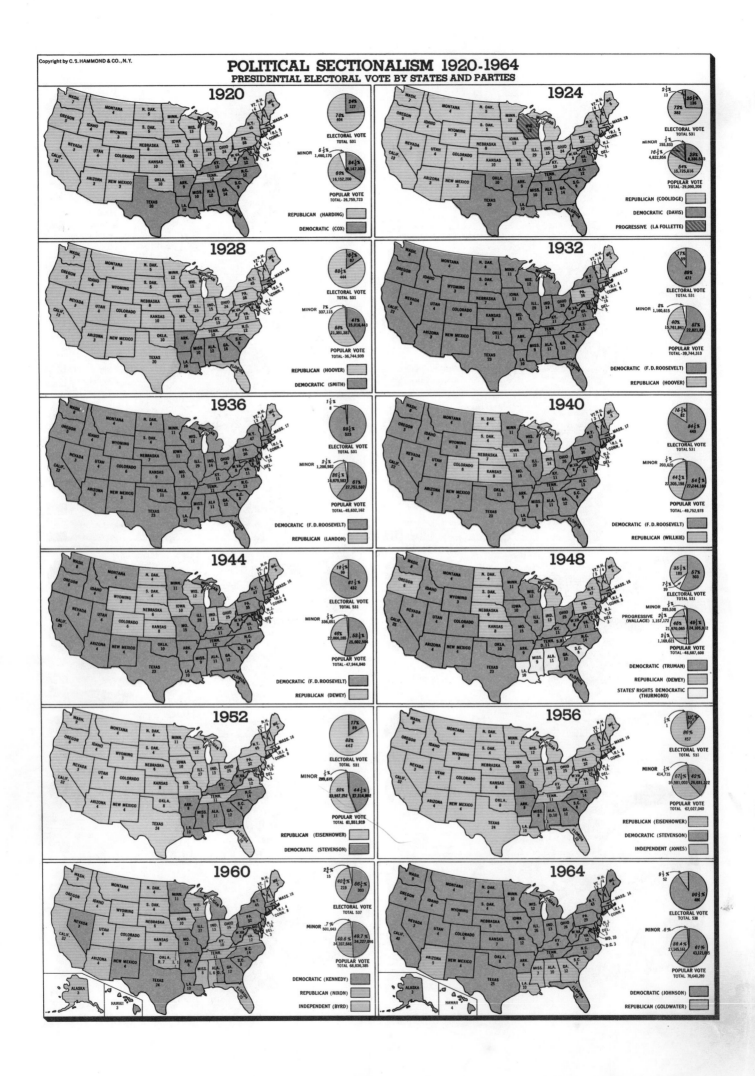

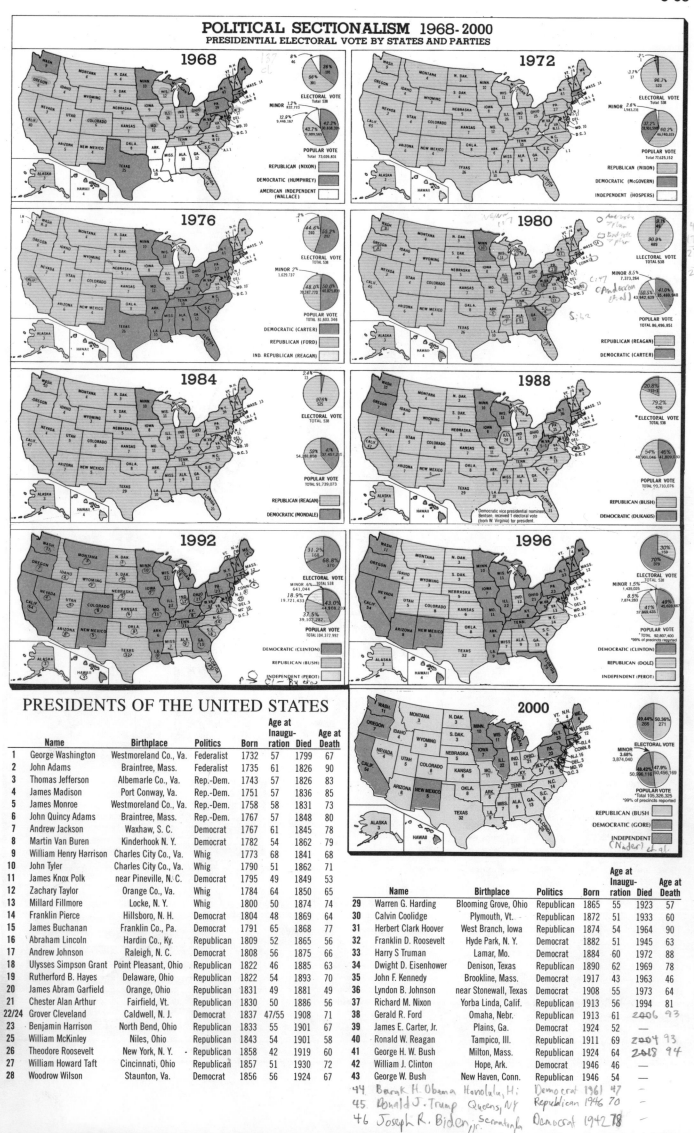

POLITICAL SECTIONALISM 1968-2000
PRESIDENTIAL ELECTORAL VOTE BY STATES AND PARTIES

1968

ELECTORAL VOTE Total 538

POPULAR VOTE Total 73,026,831

REPUBLICAN (NIXON)

DEMOCRATIC (HUMPHREY)

AMERICAN INDEPENDENT (WALLACE)

1972

ELECTORAL VOTE Total 538

POPULAR VOTE Total 77,625,152

REPUBLICAN (NIXON)

DEMOCRATIC (McGOVERN)

INDEPENDENT (HOSPERS)

1976

ELECTORAL VOTE TOTAL 538

POPULAR VOTE TOTAL 81,602,346

DEMOCRATIC (CARTER)

REPUBLICAN (FORD)

IND. REPUBLICAN (REAGAN)

1980

ELECTORAL VOTE TOTAL 538

POPULAR VOTE TOTAL 86,496,851

REPUBLICAN (REAGAN)

DEMOCRATIC (CARTER)

1984

ELECTORAL VOTE TOTAL 538

POPULAR VOTE TOTAL 91,739,073

REPUBLICAN (REAGAN)

DEMOCRATIC (MONDALE)

1988

*ELECTORAL VOTE TOTAL 538

POPULAR VOTE TOTAL 90,710,076

*Democratic vice presidential nominee, Bentsen, received 1 electoral vote (from W. Virginia) for president.

REPUBLICAN (BUSH)

DEMOCRATIC (DUKAKIS)

1992

ELECTORAL VOTE TOTAL 538

POPULAR VOTE TOTAL 104,372,992

DEMOCRATIC (CLINTON)

REPUBLICAN (BUSH)

INDEPENDENT (PEROT)

1996

ELECTORAL VOTE TOTAL 538

POPULAR VOTE *TOTAL 92,807,400 *99% of precincts reported

DEMOCRATIC (CLINTON)

REPUBLICAN (DOLE)

INDEPENDENT (PEROT)

2000

ELECTORAL VOTE

POPULAR VOTE TOTAL 105,326,325 *99% of precincts reported

REPUBLICAN (BUSH)

DEMOCRATIC (GORE)

INDEPENDENT (Nader)

PRESIDENTS OF THE UNITED STATES

	Name	Birthplace	Politics	Born	Age at Inauguration	Died	Age at Death
1	George Washington	Westmoreland Co., Va.	Federalist	1732	57	1799	67
2	John Adams	Braintree, Mass.	Federalist	1735	61	1826	90
3	Thomas Jefferson	Albemarle Co., Va.	Rep.-Dem.	1743	57	1826	83
4	James Madison	Port Conway, Va.	Rep.-Dem.	1751	57	1836	85
5	James Monroe	Westmoreland Co., Va.	Rep.-Dem.	1758	58	1831	73
6	John Quincy Adams	Braintree, Mass.	Rep.-Dem.	1767	57	1848	80
7	Andrew Jackson	Waxhaw, S. C.	Democrat	1767	61	1845	78
8	Martin Van Buren	Kinderhook N. Y.	Democrat	1782	54	1862	79
9	William Henry Harrison	Charles City Co., Va.	Whig	1773	68	1841	68
10	John Tyler	Charles City Co., Va.	Whig	1790	51	1862	71
11	James Knox Polk	near Pineville, N. C.	Democrat	1795	49	1849	53
12	Zachary Taylor	Orange Co., Va.	Whig	1784	64	1850	65
13	Millard Fillmore	Locke, N. Y.	Whig	1800	50	1874	74
14	Franklin Pierce	Hillsboro, N. H.	Democrat	1804	48	1869	64
15	James Buchanan	Franklin Co., Pa.	Democrat	1791	65	1868	77
16	Abraham Lincoln	Hardin Co., Ky.	Republican	1809	52	1865	56
17	Andrew Johnson	Raleigh, N. C.	Democrat	1808	56	1875	66
18	Ulysses Simpson Grant	Point Pleasant, Ohio	Republican	1822	46	1885	63
19	Rutherford B. Hayes	Delaware, Ohio	Republican	1822	54	1893	70
20	James Abram Garfield	Orange, Ohio	Republican	1831	49	1881	49
21	Chester Alan Arthur	Fairfield, Vt.	Republican	1830	50	1886	56
22/24	Grover Cleveland	Caldwell, N. J.	Democrat	1837	47/55	1908	71
23	Benjamin Harrison	North Bend, Ohio	Republican	1833	55	1901	67
25	William McKinley	Niles, Ohio	Republican	1843	54	1901	58
26	Theodore Roosevelt	New York, N. Y.	Republican	1858	42	1919	60
27	William Howard Taft	Cincinnati, Ohio	Republican	1857	51	1930	72
28	Woodrow Wilson	Staunton, Va.	Democrat	1856	56	1924	67

	Name	Birthplace	Politics	Born	Age at Inauguration	Died	Age at Death
29	Warren G. Harding	Blooming Grove, Ohio	Republican	1865	55	1923	57
30	Calvin Coolidge	Plymouth, Vt.	Republican	1872	51	1933	60
31	Herbert Clark Hoover	West Branch, Iowa	Republican	1874	54	1964	90
32	Franklin D. Roosevelt	Hyde Park, N. Y.	Democrat	1882	51	1945	63
33	Harry S Truman	Lamar, Mo.	Democrat	1884	60	1972	88
34	Dwight D. Eisenhower	Denison, Texas	Republican	1890	62	1969	78
35	John F. Kennedy	Brookline, Mass.	Democrat	1917	43	1963	46
36	Lyndon B. Johnson	near Stonewall, Texas	Democrat	1908	55	1973	64
37	Richard M. Nixon	Yorba Linda, Calif.	Republican	1913	56	1994	81
38	Gerald R. Ford	Omaha, Nebr.	Republican	1913	61	2006	93
39	James E. Carter, Jr.	Plains, Ga.	Democrat	1924	52	—	
40	Ronald W. Reagan	Tampico, Ill.	Republican	1911	69	2004	93
41	George H. W. Bush	Milton, Mass.	Republican	1924	64	2018	94
42	William J. Clinton	Hope, Ark.	Democrat	1946	46	—	
43	George W. Bush	New Haven, Conn.	Republican	1946	54	—	
44	Barak H. Obama	Honolulu, Hi.	Democrat	1961	47	—	
45	Ronald J. Trump	Queens, NY	Republican	1946	70	—	
46	Joseph R. Biden, jr.	Scranton, Pa	Democrat	1942	78	—	

Flags of American History

FLAGS OF DISCOVERY AND SETTLEMENT

FLAG OF LEIF ERICKSON—1000
RAVEN OF THE VIKINGS, FIRST FLAG CARRIED TO AMERICA'S SHORES.

EXPEDITIONARY FLAG OF COLUMBUS 1492

FLAG OF COLUMBUS 1492–1498
STANDARD OF FERDINAND AND ISABELLA. RAISED AT SAN SALVADOR 1492, MAINLAND, 1498.

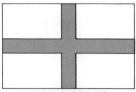

FLAG OF JOHN CABOT—1497
CROSS OF ST. GEORGE. FIRST FLAG RAISED ON MAINLAND. RALEIGH'S FLAG 1585.

FLAG OF CHAMPLAIN—1603
BORNE BY CARTIER, JOLIET, MARQUETTE, LA SALLE AND OTHER INTREPID FRENCH VOYAGEURS.

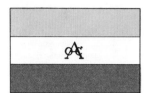

FLAG OF HUDSON—1607
FIRST FLAG RAISED AT NEW YORK. VERRAZANO DISCOVERED THE RIVER EIGHTY FOUR YEARS EARLIER.

FLAG OF THE MAYFLOWER—1620
FLAG BORNE ON THE MAIN MAST OF THE MAYFLOWER BY THE PILGRIM FATHERS.

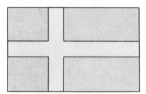

FLAG OF SWEDEN—1638
ENSIGN OF NEW SWEDEN RAISED ON THE DELAWARE RIVER.

FLAGS OF COLONIAL DAYS

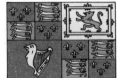

STUART STANDARD 1603–1649, 1660–1689

CROMWELL'S STANDARD 1653–1660

ROYAL STANDARD 1689–1702

ROYAL STANDARD 1707–1714

ROYAL STANDARD 1714–1801

ENGLISH RED ENSIGN
THE FAMOUS METEOR FLAG OF OLD ENGLAND AND ENSIGN OF COLONIES 17th CENTURY.

ENDICOTT FLAG—1634
THE SALEM ENSIGN SHOWING RELIGIOUS OPPOSITION TO CROSS IN CANTON.

THREE COUNTY TROUP—1659
FLAG OF THE THREE MASSACHUSETTS COUNTIES AND EMBLEM OF KING PHILIP'S WAR, 1675–1676.

ESCUTCHEONED JACK-1701
FLAG DESIGNED FOR MERCHANT SHIPS OF HIS MAJESTY'S PLANTATIONS.

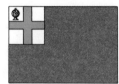

NEW ENGLAND FLAG—1737
THIS ENSIGN SHOWS THE EARLY TENDENCY OF THE COLONIES TO FIND INDIVIDUAL FLAGS.

FLAGS OF THE REVOLUTION

TAUNTON FLAG—1774
ONE OF THE EARLIEST EMBLEMS OF THE REVOLUTION.

BEDFORD FLAG—1775
CARRIED BY REVERE AND DAWES IN AROUSING THE MINUTE MEN.

CULPEPER FLAG—1775
ONE OF THE EARLY RATTLESNAKE FLAGS CARRIED BY THE MINUTE MEN.

PHILADELPHIA LIGHT HORSE
WASHINGTON'S ESCORT TO COMMAND OF THE CONTINENTAL ARMY, 1775.

RHODE ISLAND FLAG—1776
CARRIED AT BRANDYWINE, TRENTON AND YORKTOWN.

FORT MOULTRIE FLAG—1776
NAILED TO STAFF BY SERGEANT JASPER WHEN SHOT AWAY.

LIBERTY TREE FLAG—1776
THE PINE TREE COMES FROM COINS OF THE COLONY OF MASSACHUSETTS, 1652.

BENNINGTON FLAG—1777
FLAG OF VICTORY OF THE GREEN MOUNTAIN BOYS.

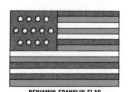

BENJAMIN FRANKLIN FLAG
ALSO CALLED "SERAPIS" FLAG. GENERALLY ACCEPTED AS ORIGINATED BY BENJAMIN FRANKLIN AT COURT OF LOUIS XVI.

MERCHANT ENSIGN 1776–1795
AN EMBLEM IN GENERAL USE, ALSO PRIVATEER'S FLAG.

FLAGS OF THE OLD NAVY

GADSDEN FLAG—1775
COMMODORE ESEK HOPKINS' ENSIGN USED IN HIS FIRST FLEET COMMAND.

WASHINGTON'S NAVY ENSIGN—1775
THE FLAG OF THE SIX CRUISERS THAT FORMED THE FIRST AMERICAN NAVAL FLEET.

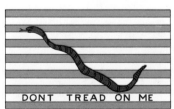

FIRST NAVY JACK—1775
HOSTED AT THE MAIN MAST BY COMMANDER-IN-CHIEF ESEK HOPKINS, DECEMBER 3, 1775.

FLAGS OF THE YOUNG REPUBLIC

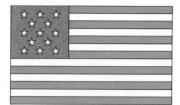

FIRST NAVY STARS AND STRIPES
IN ABSENCE OF SPECIFIC ARRANGEMENT OF STARS BY CONGRESS JUNE 14, 1777
IT WAS CUSTOMARY FOR NAVY TO PLACE THE STARS IN FORM OF CROSSES OF
ST. GEORGE AND ST. ANDREW.

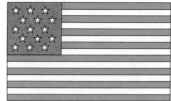

"STAR SPANGLED BANNER" —1814
THE EMBLEM OF INSPIRATION OF OUR NATIONAL ANTHEM, 1814.
FLAG OF VICTORY OVER BARBARY PIRATES 1803 TO 1805.

FREMONT THE PATHFINDER'S FLAG—40'S
EMBLEM THAT BLAZED THE TRAIL FOR THE COVERED WAGON
IN THE ROARING 40'S. THE EARLY ENSIGN OF THE PLAINS.

FAMOUS BATTLE FLAGS

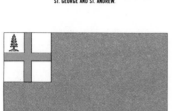

BUNKER HILL FLAG—1775
HISTORIC EMBLEM THAT PROVED THE STRENGTH OF THE SPIRIT
OF AMERICAN LIBERTY. CARRIED AT LEXINGTON AND CONCORD.

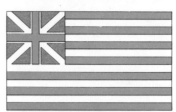

CAMBRIDGE FLAG, FIRST NAVY ENSIGN 1775–1776
HOISTED BY JOHN PAUL JONES, DECEMBER 3, 1775 AND BY
GENERAL WASHINGTON, JANUARY 2, 1776.

CONTINENTAL FLAG
CARRIED IN 1775–1777, SHOWING PINE TREE, SYMBOL OF
MASSACHUSETTS BAY COLONY, IN PLACE OF THE CROSSES OF
ST. GEORGE AND ST. ANDREW.

FLAGS OF THE CONFEDERACY

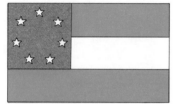

FIRST CONFEDERATE FLAG
FAMOUS "STARS AND BARS" USED FROM MARCH 1861 TO MAY 1863.

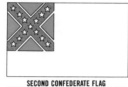

SECOND CONFEDERATE FLAG
NATIONAL EMBLEM FROM MAY 1, 1863 TO MARCH 4, 1865.

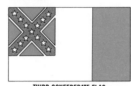

THIRD CONFEDERATE FLAG
NATIONAL EMBLEM ADOPTED MARCH 8, 1865.

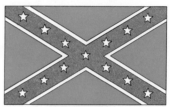

CONFEDERATE NAVY FLAG
USED FROM MAY 1, 1863 TO END OF WAR, 1865.
THE BATTLE FLAG WAS SQUARE.

OTHER NOTEWORTHY FLAGS OF AMERICAN HISTORY

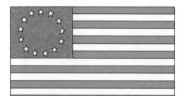

FIRST STARS AND STRIPES
UNITED EMBLEM OF INDEPENDENCE SAID TO HAVE ORIGINATED BY
GEORGE WASHINGTON FOLLOWING ACT OF CONGRESS OF JUNE 14, 1777.

PRESENT DAY FLAG

"OLD GLORY"
NAME GIVEN BY CAPTAIN WILLIAM DRIVER, COMMANDING THE BRIG
"CHARLES DAGGETT" IN 1831.

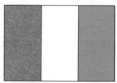

FLAG OF THE THIRD MARYLAND REGIMENT—1778
CARRIED AT THE BATTLE OF COWPENS JANUARY, 1778 AND USED AS COLORS OF
AMERICAN LAND FORCES UNTIL MEXICAN WAR.

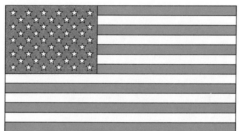

NAPOLEON'S LOUISIANA FLAG
THIS FLAG WAS REPLACED BY "STARS AND STRIPES"
FOLLOWING LOUISIANA PURCHASE DECEMBER 24, 1803.

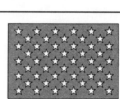

U.S. NAVY JACK
USED BY NAVAL VESSELS AND
MARITIME GOVERNORS.

FLAG OF THE MEXICAN WAR—1845
NOT ACTUALLY USED AS REGIMENTAL COLORS BY TROOPS, BUT AS FLAG
OF CONQUEST AND OCCUPATION.

FLAG OF THE WAR OF 1812 (1812–1814)
SHOWING FIFTEEN STARS AND FIFTEEN BARS AS CHANGED UPON
ADMISSION OF VERMONT.

RUSSIAN AMERICAN CO'S. FLAG
EMBLEM RAISED 1799, REPLACED BY
"STARS AND STRIPES" 1867.

U.S. COAST GUARD FLAG
WITHOUT EMBLEM ON FLY THIS IS
U.S. CUSTOMS FLAG.

FLAG OF THE CIVIL WAR 1861–1865
THE "STARS AND STRIPES" WITH THIRTY SIX STARS IN THE UNION CARRIED
BY THE NORTHERN ARMIES DURING LATER YEARS OF THE CIVIL WAR.

THE FLAG OF 1818
SHOWING RETURN TO THIRTEEN STRIPES AND ADDITIONAL STARS IN CANTON.

COMMODORE PERRY'S FLAG—1854
THE FLAG THAT OPENED JAPAN
TO WESTERN CIVILIZATION.

AMERICAN YACHT ENSIGN
AUTHORIZED BY ACT OF CONGRESS
AUGUST 7, 1848.

FLAG OF THE SPANISH-AMERICAN WAR—1898
THE EMBLEM OF LIBERTY THAT BROUGHT FREEDOM TO CUBA.

Flags of States, Territories and Possessions

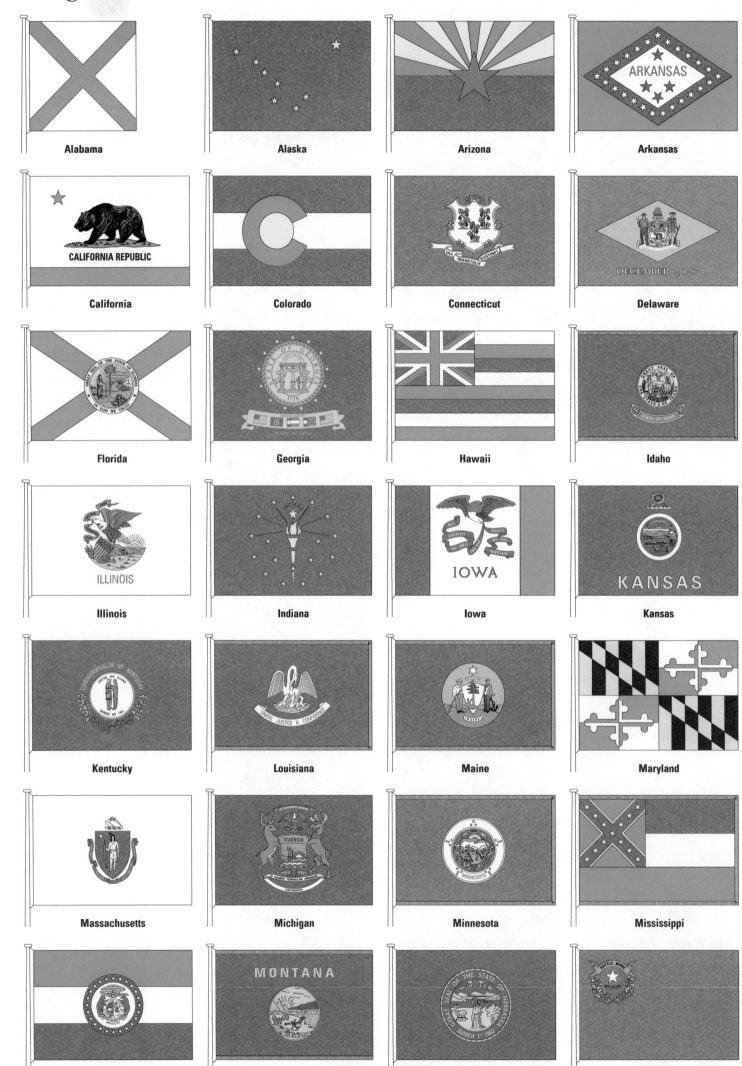

Alabama

Alaska

Arizona

Arkansas

California

Colorado

Connecticut

Delaware

Florida

Georgia

Hawaii

Idaho

Illinois

Indiana

Iowa

Kansas

Kentucky

Louisiana

Maine

Maryland

Massachusetts

Michigan

Minnesota

Mississippi

Missouri

Montana

Nebraska

Nevada

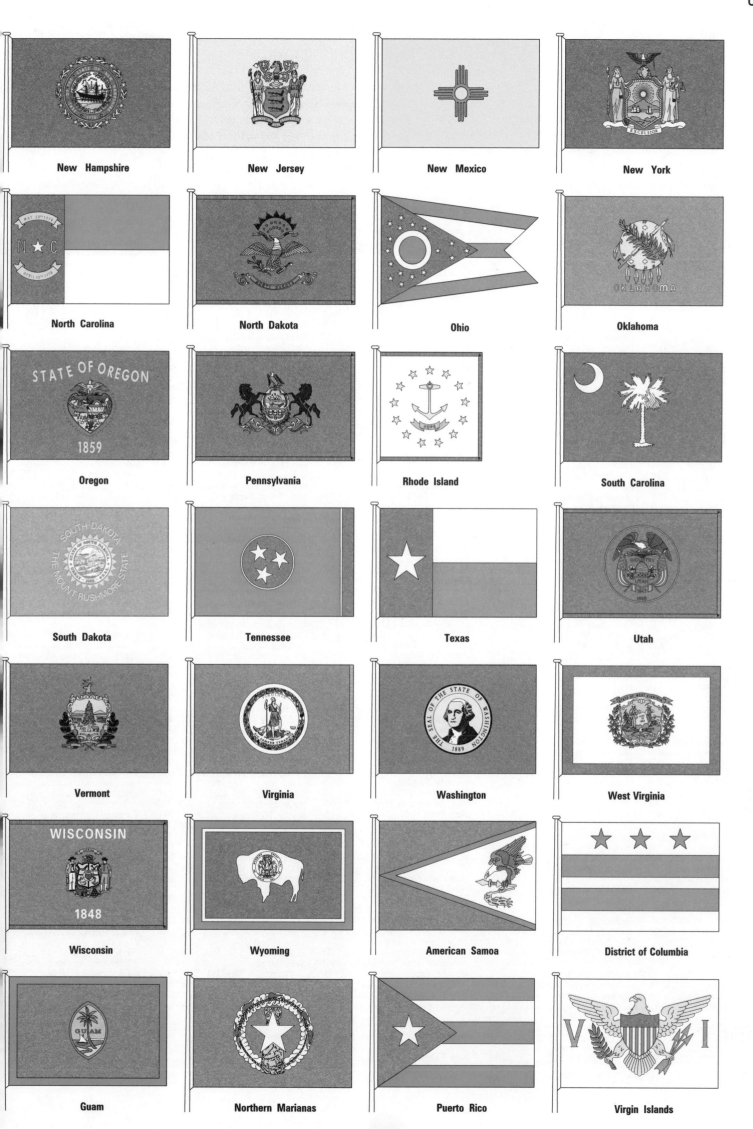

New Hampshire

New Jersey

New Mexico

New York

North Carolina

North Dakota

Ohio

Oklahoma

Oregon

Pennsylvania

Rhode Island

South Carolina

South Dakota

Tennessee

Texas

Utah

Vermont

Virginia

Washington

West Virginia

Wisconsin

Wyoming

American Samoa

District of Columbia

Guam

Northern Marianas

Puerto Rico

Virgin Islands

Index

This index lists historically important places, areas, events and geographical features appearing on the maps of the United States History Atlas. Each entry is followed by the page number on which the name appears. The letters following the page number designate a particular map on pages containing more than one map. Names that appear on more than one map are indexed to the map or maps portraying the place at its most historically significant period.